Joseph Edkins

Modern China

Thirty-one Short Essays on Subjects Which Illustrate the Present...

Joseph Edkins

Modern China
Thirty-one Short Essays on Subjects Which Illustrate the Present...

ISBN/EAN: 9783337003944

Printed in Europe, USA, Canada, Australia, Japan

Cover: Foto ©ninafisch / pixelio.de

More available books at **www.hansebooks.com**

MODERN CHINA:

THIRTY-ONE SHORT ESSAYS ON SUBJECTS WHICH ILLUSTRATE

THE PRESENT CONDITION OF THE COUNTRY.

BY

JOSEPH EDKINS, D.D.

SHANGHAI:
SOLD BY KELLY & WALSH, LD., AND BY W. BREWER.

LONDON:
SOLD BY TRÜBNER & Co., LUDGATE STREET

1891.

INDEX.

MODERN CHINA.

THE NUMERICAL INCREASE OF THE CHINESE RACE.

THE rapid growth of the United States in population is due to immigration as well as to the industrial prosperity of the country. But in China there is no great infusion of outside races to aid in accounting for the remarkable increase of the population of this country since the reign of Kang-hi. The rapid growth of the people in numbers is due to industrious habits, to mild and paternal government, to the extension of trade and the effect also of the intellectual vigour of the people. If any one should attempt to account for the swift growth of India in numbers and wealth, the political and commercial causes would be set down as the most energetic of the forces which give to the decennial census in that country its wonderful spring upwards. The vessel of the state is there guided with a firm hand, and robbery and violence are kept in restraint. Railways and convenient seaports allow of a rapid increase in those products of India which are suitable for foreign markets; and those articles of European make which India will buy are cheaply conveyed to every inland city. Such are the chief causes of the increase in the number of the Hindoo population. But in addition to these there is also the subdivision of occupations; the religious castes, the merchants, the inferior castes and all the varieties of Hindoo social distinctions tend to increase the population and operate against emigration. If there must be a separate person to do everything and make every article that Hindoo life requires, there will be in each community some one to do that particular thing. This increases the population so far, and the check is found in the limitation of the means of living.

So it is in China. Foreign trade has increased the growth of silk; and with that the number of mulberry tree tenders, of silk worm feeders, of spinners and weavers, of retail and wholesale merchants has increased in proportion. Out of the 380 millions of China, if we adopt the native census, as we are compelled to do for want of a better, we may roughly estimate the number of persons engaged exclusively in agriculture as 38 millions, or one in ten. One Chinaman in a hundred is a bricklayer or mason. The blacksmiths are one in 140. One in a hundred and twenty is a tailor. The washerman is quite as commonly to be met with. A carpenter is to be seen in every hundredth man. Something like this is the proportion in England, and it may serve us for a convenient comparison. In England, in the census lists there are about a hundred divisions of occupations, and there are nearly as many in China. Of course there are some Chinese occupations which have nothing corresponding to them in Europe; and some professions, astrologers for example, which it is a rare thing to meet with in England, abound in China. It is to be noted that, supposing the occupations of the Chinese to be about a hundred, each adds to the population its own percentage; and when food and clothing, with the etceteras, are to be had there will be some one engaged in that occupation in every community. But if they cannot be had because the people have grown poor and do not need such a person, he moves to a place of larger population. Thus small places grow smaller and large places larger. The subdivision of occupations is a powerful force in increasing the population; and the principal limit which so operates as to check the rate of growth is the quantity of food produced.

The question has been asked, What have been the chief causes of that still increasing energy of the Chinese race which enables them to absorb other nations and always be found conquering in the struggle for existence? The population tables shew that they did not grow at any time beyond about 60 millions until, at the end of the 17th century, the great body politic began to assume gigantic proportions. This growth has continued in the face of famines, wars and pestilences, and it now causes that overflow which in the United States and Australia occasions a serious political disquietude. The causes appear to be the absence of vexatious interference with the people by the government, the extension of foreign trade, the effects of stimulus given to education by the examinations, and the spread of emigration. As to the government, the two reigns Kang-hi and Chien-lung both lasted sixty years and the wars undertaken were then always successful. The laws were ameliorated, the poll tax, which acted as a check on population, was abolished, and the people were allowed to have their own way to such an extent that it may be said that China is democratic, while in theory ruled by a despotic government. The upward movement of population was delayed in the Kang-hi period by the wars with Wu San-kwei and Koxinga, but as soon as universal tranquillity was restored the increase indicated by the census returns shewed that political peace is the great thing required by the Chinese race to ensure its prosperity.

Another powerful cause is found in the educational system. The encouragement given to literature by the government reaches to every village throughout this vast country. The number of schoolmasters, doctors, secretaries to mandarins, caligraphists and a host of other professions is thus greatly increased, over and above the places secured in the mandarinate high and low by students successful in the high examinations. Foreign trade has also been a substantial cause of numerical growth during the present dynasty, because it has increased greatly the number of merchants, burden bearers, and silk and tea cultivators. Lastly, emigration encourages population in a remarkable degree. In China as in England the places of those who leave are soon filled up ; and when emigrants return rich the wealth they bring operates powerfully to increase the population, because it is used as capital in adding to local industries.

THE TEMPLE OF HEAVEN.

On the 10th September, 1889, the Temple of Heaven was destroyed by fire and the cause was its being struck by lightning. The building thus destroyed is the Chinien-tien which stands on the northern altar. It was 99 feet high and had a triple blue roof which was elaborately repaired a century ago. It differed from Buddhist pagodas because the roofs were circular, and one above another. The very striking appearance of this edifice has led many visitors to regard it as the most sacred part of the erections embraced in the Temple of Heaven. Yet in fact the south altar without any edifice built on it is the most primitive and in some sense more sacred. There is no very clear classical precedent for the building over the altar which has now been destroyed. The altar is essential. The edifice over it is a later addition and does not certainly date from a time earlier than A.D. 483. In that year at Nanking, then the capital of South China, there was a discussion at court as to whether a roofed building should be erected on the altar for the spring sacrifice or not. There never was a question as to the south altar where sacrifices are offered at the solstices whether a temple should be built on it or not. It was thought more reverential to worship at an open altar. But in reference to the spring sacrifice it was decided that a building might be allowed. "If in the ancestral temple of the Emperors" said one of the courtiers " the round tent there used at sacrifices has been changed into a temple and carpets spread there, why should not the same be done at the Altar of Heaven?" Another remarked that the law-book of antiquity, the Chow Li, certainly spoke of felt carpets and it was therefore probable that there was a house. The Emperor approved. The opposition was silenced, and a temple was built, to be used in the first month of the calendar, when at the opening of spring the Emperor leaves his palace to pray for a fruitful year. In this temple there was space to arrange the tablets of the emperor's ancestors as assessors with the tablet of the Supreme Ruler of the Universe. In this way the imperial tablets on the east and west shared in the banquet of the sacrifices with the Supreme Ruler. The day was after the sixth of February each year on the first occurrence of the character *hsin*, "new" the eighth in the series of ten names attached to days. That the lofty blue-roofed temple now destroyed should at all have a secondary character in the Imperial worship may seem in itself unlikely, but it must be remembered that the ancient Chinese idea of the worship of the Supreme requires simplicity and humility with reverence. Thus a temple having a beautifully coloured roof covered with glazed tiles, having blue, yellow, and green paint under the glaze, or blue only, is not allowed on the round altar where worship is performed at the winter solstice. The chief of all the sacrifices is that of the 21st of December and this has nothing to do with the temple now destroyed. It will be performed as usual.

The next occasion when the burnt temple would have been used will be in February of 1890. If it should be decided not to rebuild the temple the round altar on which it stood is still there with its beauty of carved marble balustrades and flights of marble steps. The ceremonies as in the time before A.D. 483 can be performed in their full splendour. It would be a return to antiquity ; it would be paying honour to

the ritual of the ancient Emperors not to rebuild the temple at all, but to perform the great national act of worship for the commencement of spring on the open altar as at the altar where the sacrifices of June and December are offered. Next February, as a matter of necessity, this will be done. The ruins of the beautiful structure of the Ming dynasty will be removed, and new shrines and tablets for the Imperial line of deceased Emperors will be prepared. The ritual will be the same. The carefully selected bullock will be consumed by fire in the furnace altar on the south east as before. The Emperor will kneel on the round centre stone of the altar to prostrate himself before the tablet as his ancestors have done at the southern altar for two centuries and a half, and the retinue of two thousand persons will be there as usual on these occasions. The slaughtered bullocks, one in honour of each Emperor worshipped, will be placed in order before the tablets. The prayer will be read and burnt that it may fly upward in smoke and flame to the azure sky. Only the magnificence of the temple now destroyed will be wanting, and this is not essential to the completeness of the worship.

The best course to be pursued would be for the Councillors of the Emperor to study history on this point. If they find that the temple was first erected on the altar in the time of Ch'i Wu-ti whose dynasty only lasted twenty-three years and only ruled South China, they might see reason not to rebuild it. If however it should be rebuilt, it will be the work of years, because three circles of teak pillars of the largest kind, those of one circle being ninety feet high, are required to support the three roofs and the conveyance of these from Yünnan will occupy much time. In view of the opening of the railway from Peking to Hankow, the fire is unfortunate because it will give strength to the enemies of progress. They will after this fire make new efforts to stay the hand of the government in prosecuting this enterprise. The effect of this catastrophe on the minds of the Imperial family will be most painful. Those among the statesmen of China at present who are friendly to progress will be much impeded in their endeavours to promote the prosperity of their country. In time-honoured theory this beautiful temple, which can only be seen now in pictures and photographs, is connected by inseparable links with the safety of the dynasty, but this view may be shaken and modified by this very occurrence. It is to be hoped that some Censor may suggest that the fire is to be interpreted as indicating other things rather than danger from railways, and that one chief lesson to be learned from it is the need of lightning conductors to preserve Chinese high buildings from the thunderbolt of destruction. The Court is however more inclined to take the incident as an indication of the displeasure of Heaven at the negligence of officials in charge of the sacred building.

NEED OF TREE PLANTING IN NORTH-CHINA.

THE desiccation of North-China which has now rendered it much more liable than the south and west to the destructive effects of famine is due among other things to the general cutting down of trees. The excess of population renders individuals poorer and subdivides the land into lots which are too small for the decent maintenance of a family, and when drought comes trees rapidly disappear because the inhabitants are too poor to buy fuel. Every time of drought leads to a vast destruction of vegetable life for fuel, and the restorative power of nature cannot compensate for it in sufficient time, because the number of human beings needing vegetable matter to burn is too great. Ku Yen-wu tells us that North-China was formerly rich in bamboos, so that when an embankment had to be made in Chang-te prefecture in the extreme north of Honan province bamboos were used to strengthen it. Much difficulty

and delay were caused lately previous to the closing of the Chengchou gap in the Yellow River embankment by want of sufficient millet stalks. In ancient times bamboos were forthcoming in sufficient quantity and of course were more serviceable than millet stalks, which are used now because nothing stronger can be had, to strengthen the embankments. This was in the western Han period. In the eastern Han in the time of the Emperor Kwangwu, his minister cut down more than a million bamboos to make arrows for the army which was engaged in vanquishing Wang Mang the usurper. The name of this Minister was K'ou Hsün and it is a noted name. These bamboos grew in Wei Hui prefecture. Confucius and Mencius had both visited this country a few centuries earlier. In their days the country would look well wooded. It is one of the great evils attendant on political trouble, that military necessity destroys woods and groves without mercy. Here is an instance of it. One time of anarchy needs a century to follow it before a devastated region can recover its former prosperity. Farther west, in the valley of the Wei in Shensi, a continuous grove of bamboos of a thousand mow, or 166 acres, is casually mentioned in history about B.C. 100, and the Ch'in Emperors before this had an officer styled Inspector of Bamboos. The industry of the same native author finds also allusions in various books to the bamboos which grew in Shantung in the prefecture of Tai-an Fu on the south of the Tai-shan mountain range in the Lu country, and on the north of the same range in the Ch'i country. It may be concluded then that the vegetable growth of the plains of North-China has been much diminished and the change not only greatly increases the poverty of the people, but adds also to the dryness of the atmosphere because trees draw water from the subsoil through their roots and this moisture finds its way into the air.

The Chinese are now engaged in constructing a railway from Peking to

Hankow. It is undertaken by the government and will be conducted on the joint stock principle under the direction of the Viceroys. After leaving Peking and proceeding for two hundred miles in a south-westerly direction the line will proceed in a direction nearly due south. When it reaches Chang-te, four hundred miles from Peking and Wei-hwei 470 miles from the same city, it will be passing through the same region where large groves of bamboos and other trees once beautified the face of the land and moistened the air. It would be a wise act, a benefit likely to prove of incalculable value, if in connection with the railway now to be constructed, the Governor of Honan, a man of tried energy and large knowledge, should take measures to restore the former aspect of the country in those portions of his province which border on the new railway and on the Yellow River. The benefits derivable from tree plantations are manifold. The railway will always need wood for consumption. The Yellow River always needs wood or bamboo for strengthening the embankments; bamboo groves would supply northern markets with poles for burden bearers and for the scaffolding which is required everywhere to erect lofty awnings for marriage feasts and funerals, and for coolness in all large houses in summer. Possibly the climate during the twenty centuries that have elapsed has seriously deteriorated. Even in this case bamboos could be cultivated in sheltered situations. If protected from cold winds by poplar or other plantations more hardy than bamboo they would be likely to flourish. If grown in localities where there was a city wall to windward, or on the south and south-west of mountains their chance would be still more improved. For tree planting the lee side of mountains and hills is to be preferred, but the broad plains of Chihli, Honan and Shantung must have plantations of trees also, because the air there is too dry and trees, while they equalise the rainfall when it occurs, increase the evaporation which moistens the atmos-

phere in dry seasons. On the south side of every high embankment and city wall, there should be trees planted to be under the care of a special department assisted by the officers who have charge of the Yellow River and of the local authorities of every city. It is to be hoped that Ni Wên-wei, the Honan Governor, will do this in his province and that the Viceroys, Li and Chang, will also become aware that the construction of this great railway affords a most favourable opportunity of securing many excellent sites for tree planting. Certainly it is to be expected that they will welcome the idea that the wooded appearance of the country when it was looked on by the great sage in his travels ought to be restored.

THE CHINESE LANGUAGE.

THE difference between the Chinese and Japanese at the present time is plainly seen in their attitude in regard to foreign manners and habits. The Japanese are rapidly changing their costume and they have adopted a code of laws based on European legislation. They are also making great efforts to Romanise their writing and dismiss Chinese tradition from their schools. The Chinese are not at all likely to change their costume or their laws. Nor will they abandon their mode of writing. They are on the way to school improvements, and science will soon force an entrance into the literary examinations. There is a rumour that the Emperor is himself fond of mathematics and astronomy. It is likely that the new College at Tientsin erected by the Viceroy of Chihli for the scientific education of youth will be open to receive pupils in the Spring of 1890. But while the Chinese will learn science they will not for a long time to come abandon their mode of writing as the Japanese many of them would like to do. Western science is coming more to the front than it was and to know it is a necessity, but the Chinese will not tire of their own language. Many of them now learn English and afterwards they can if they choose acquire a competent knowledge of science from reading western text books. Nor will science remain shut up in European modes of speech. The Chinese language as the natives use it has great force, fluency, and directness. It is practical as the nation is practical, and those who use it are too independent to abandon the speech and writing handed down to them through so long a line of ancestors. It will be made the medium of instruction in science and is very suitable for becoming so. They have contractions for all their characters which foreign students do not trouble themselves to learn, but the use of which in fact qualifies the Chinese to become short-hand reporters of speeches in their own language. They do not practise speech making, but if they did and if the native newspapers formed a staff of short-hand reporters they would not need to learn any foreign system. They can report quite fast enough themselves with a little practice and they write the contractions with wonderful quickness. Their hand muscles are pliable, their fingers small, and the writing brush they employ is as an instrument superior in speed to the steel pen or the quill. The scribes at an imperial audience probably write all or nearly all that is said. Scribes who are paid by the piece get through a large amount of copying in a very short time. Yet let no one expect a teacher who is paid by the month to write fast. He has every reason to be slow. But copyists paid so much for a thousand characters try naturally to transcribe as many thousand in a week as they can. The rapid work of such copyists, especially if they are allowed to use contractions, favours the conclusion that by using Chinese characters specialists could easily write all that a good speaker says. As to whether they could compete with the quickest European stenographers may perhaps soon be brought to a trial in Japan, where many thousands are now learning to write in the Roman character. The new school will soon proceed to add shorthand to Romanisation and then it will soon be decided which is the best adapted for swift and accurate reporting.

The Chinese character is at present used in China, Japan, Corea and Cochin China. In all these countries the educated class express their ideas in this form. Whence did it come? Is it a purely native invention or is it of foreign origin? Let it be remembered that the old writing of China before the seal character was invented about B.C. 800 was called the "tadpole writing" from the stroke being round and thick at one end and pointed at the other. Attention was drawn to it by Kung-an-kuo a great scholar in the second century before Christ. It was on occasion of the discovery of a valuable collection of books in the house of Confucius about B.C. 150. The prince of Lu had ordered the house to be taken down, and in secret repositories in the walls several separate and complete classical works were found and entrusted to Kung-an-kuo who was head of the Confucian family at that time. In Legge's Classics in the Prolegomena to the Discourses of Confucius and to the Book of History this fortunate discovery is described. The writing looked strange because it had gone out of use. The Revolution of B.C. 220 had among the many great changes then made altered the writing too. The Han scholars therefore adopted the name K'o-tou "tadpole" to denote the strange old writing which had been common four centuries before. What is seen of the early writing in native books now is the seal character. The ancient mode of writing which Confucius used, presenting to the eye a grouping of strokes thick at the beginning and finishing with a point, the true Koo-wen, is not represented in books. If it were present to the eye the Babylonian origin of the Chinese writing would at once be obvious. What the Han scholars called tadpole shaped, we may call cuneiform writing, applied to the Chinese.

But it may be objected that the K'otou writing common in the time of Confucius was not the ancient writing seen on bells, vases and other antiquities. To this it may be replied that the Babylonians had a pre-cuneiform writing as well as the cuneiform itself. It was to a large extent ideographic and possibly the earliest Chinese writing may have been founded on the older Babylonian writing, as the tadpole script was on the new style known as the cuneiform. That the old Chinese writing seen on bells and vases was a foreign invention is probable because it is connected with an advanced knowledge of astronomy. That the mode of writing with which Confucius was familiar was the latter Babylonian is very likely, because the Chinese had in his day already begun to write numbers from left to right with strokes in the Babylonian way precisely. For example 川 ≣ 丄 川 二 丨 三 would at that time have been understood to be 89 6 4 2 1 3, both at Babylon and in China as used in both countries. In China this mode of writing numbers has been kept up till the present time as supplemental to the ten characters in ordinary use.

--- ◆ ---

FOOT BINDING.

In the Monthly Journal of the Ethnographic Society of France, there is in the number for August of the year 1889 a paper on the deformed feet of Chinese women. In 1861, M. de Fusier, a surgeon in the English and French expeditionary force which captured Peking, found the remains of a female foot in a tomb near Palikao ten miles to the east of the capital. A battle was fought there between the Chinese troops and the French and English forces. There was no one to check the examination of a tomb. The woman had been buried apparently not long before. The coffin was broken and the foot accessible. M. de Fusier found that it was impossible to preserve the soft parts of it, but he kept the bones. He published a minute account of the injuries sustained by each of the foot bones through the habit of tight bandaging, with drawings of the deformed foot and of the shoe worn by women and girls who have been subjected by the fashion of their country to this cruelty. The account appeared more than 20 years ago in a French Journal of Surgery and Medicine and on this the paper which was read before the Ethnographical Society was based. Marco Polo does not mention the tight bandaging of women's feet nor the limp of Chinese women walking as they always do, only upon the back part of the foot. In the 14th century a traveller who wrote in old French was the first European to describe this capricious deformity. His statements were brought to light by Pauthier who was an ardent archæologist in all matters connected with China. Sometimes a bone is removed to diminish the size of the growing foot more rapidly. At fifteen the bones cease to grow and it is only then that pain is no longer felt. Little girls weep from the pain of tight bandaging but the sympathising mothers think it a necessity and dare not allow their little feet to retain their natural shape. The reason that the husbands do not object to deformed feet is stated to be that they think it much better for wives to be always at home. Unfortunately women submit much too willingly to an absurd custom from a desire not to be unfashionable. Pressure on the foot bones and adjacent nerves, says the French account, tends to paralyse the thigh muscle known as the triceps, and in other ways to produce disordered action in neighbouring localities by sympathy. The women of the middle class imitate the rich and even in poor families there are some who have small feet the result of bandaging when they were children. The empress and all the Tartar ladies of the court have feet of natural size, and it need scarcely be said that no censor has ever been known to present a memorial animadverting on what from a

Chinese point of view must be considered a great irregularity.

Now as to the origin of this cruel custom, the Chinese have themselves traced it to the usages of a court in the province of Kiangsu in the tenth century. There seems to be no doubt that the conclusion arrived at by the native investigators is correct. It is, however, based not upon contemporary diaries public or private but on circumstantial evidence. Li Yi was a prince of the Imperial house of Tang who after the fall of his dynasty retained for a time a small principality and kept his court at Nanking. The city was besieged and taken in A.D. 975 by the troops of Chao Kuang-yin founder of the Sung dynasty. Too prudent to commit suicide, Li Yi allowed himself to be taken prisoner and was sent to Kai-fêng Fu, the new capital, to await the pleasure of the emperor. This prince was in good humour having now conquered the whole empire. The highborn captive was treated kindly, received a duke's title, and died in 978. At Nanking he had in his prosperity an inferior wife named Yao Niang, whose dancing pleased him much. He had a golden lotus made six feet in height in his dancing hall. It would be of stucco work gilt. Through the interstices of the flower was seen the new moon shining among floating clouds of many colours. Li Yi wished the feet of Yao Niang while dancing to look like the new moon. He commanded her therefore to bind her feet with silk bandages so as to bend them into a shape like the new moon. This became the type of Chinese beauty in the feet. The front part of the sole is forcibly bent downwards, four of the toes are bent under the sole, and the whole foot assumes the appearance of a curve like the new moon. This custom by following which nine-tenths of the women of China have to endure the pain of tight bandaging from seven years of age to fourteen or fifteen, really began in this way. A man whom history condemns as hesitating and incapable, and

of whom no good and worthy actions are recorded, became the founder of this capricious fashion. He wished his favourite wife when dancing before him to represent in her dress the clouds of the evening sky and coloured as they are coloured, and in her feet the moon. A poet addressed to her one of his compositions and from the expressions he uses it is concluded that the custom of foot bandaging really commenced with her. The desire to have extremely small feet curved like the moon became a mania which from Nanking spread over the whole empire gradually. So imperceptible was the movement and so entirely the effect of fashion unaided and unimpeded by any imperial decree, that the historians took no notice of it and left it to poets and painters as a part of their sphere to preserve the record as to how and when it began. The French account exaggerates the evils resulting to the system from the cramping of the fore-foot and the destruction to a larger or smaller extent of its bones, nerves, and muscles. Evidence for these evil results on the system generally among the Chinese themselves is not forthcoming. In saying too that infants are thus tormented the French statements are wrong, but the astonishing fact remains that for nine centuries the women of China have submitted to all this pain and to this deprivation of freedom in motion for the sake of having a beautiful foot and because of the tyranny of fashion. This country has great need of enlightened views on medicine and on the anatomy of the human frame. It needs also teaching in true art that the people may learn in what real beauty consists. The men are to blame for not enlightening the women on these points and the women are greatly to blame for allowing little girls of seven and eight years old to be subjected, with or without their own will, to this perfectly unnecessary torture.

THE ART OF CHINA AND JAPAN.

"THE Paris Exhibition of 1889 has revealed Japan as the first nation in the art of decoration. It is at the feet of the Japanese Gamaliels that the men of the West seek inspiration, to apply art to industry." Such is the view of the correspondent of the *North-China Daily News* writing October 19, 1889, and he probably gives the opinion which he heard commonly expressed in the French capital.

This must mean that Japanese workmen have an eye for the arrangement of colour and for artistic grouping as well as a perception of the beauty of forms such as the European cannot equal. It is a sign of the times that Chinese and Japanese art are in the view of European criticism destined to enlarge our acquaintance with the beautiful. Atkinson's works have shown that China and Japan help to fill up certain vacant places in the sphere of art. This need not surprise us, for patient labour conquers all difficulties. *Labor omnia vincit improbus.* Such patient working, carried on for a long period by a large number of skilled workers, is sure to be rewarded occasionally by the impulses of genius which come at one time or another quite uncertainly to some favoured person, who then by his work in carving or grouping convinces observers that he is endowed with "the vision and the faculty divine."

It has been the happy fortune of European nations to be to each other stimulating neighbours for many successive centuries in matters relating to art. When Italy obtained deep glimpses into the world of beauty through her great painters and sculptors, all Europe reaped the benefit. Our own English artists of repute were able to attain higher excellence in their ideal compositions because, by studying great paintings, they practically placed themselves under the instruction of the men of genius who produced them. European excellence in art has been great in proportion to the amount of good influence thus exerted in each century

on students by the works of their predecessors in their own and neighbouring countries. Ideas in design, beautiful effects in grouping and the introduction of every sort of improvement in materials and workmanship are easily imitated when the worker has them before him, and so the progress of one nation becomes the progress of many. But it is perfectly possible that certain fashions may rule for a time and may have a limiting effect on the advance of the æsthetic student. European art has not penetrated into every region of the universe of beauty. Results still remain to be achieved because fashion has held back the aspiring student and forced him by its influence into certain paths where he could attain a temporary popularity. He has been kept from pursuing certain other paths where new beauties would have rewarded his efforts because the suggestion was wanting. The Japanese and Chinese artists have been working for centuries in a world of their own and derived suggestions from other sources than those of Europe. Their art is Buddhistic instead of being Christian. The power of the Christian faith in elevating the sphere of European art is shewn in the works of the Italian painters. The greatest men of genius in the West have chosen Christian subjects as richer than any other in æsthetic suggestiveness. Nowhere could they find such examples of moral purity and aspiring spirituality of thought as were presented in Christianity. This religion elevated the powers of the great painters as nothing else has ever done. Sympathy with their favourite subjects gave to Raphael and Domenichino their undoubted superiority in their delineation of beauty in the realm of art. The artists of China and Japan never had these special advantages. Indian art is essentially grotesque and these artists trained under Buddhism were obliged to work therefore very much on grotesque subjects. So also it is with the mythology of the genii in China. An old man with an exaggerated head sitting under a tree with a crooked staff beside him, or riding on a cow, is to them a subject of high art. They wish to glorify old age and they draw it in the form of one of the genii, who, with the deep lines of age upon his face, looks contentedly upon a bright sky above or on the waters of a river flowing past him. Such is the limited height to which Chinese art can attain, because the vision of the Christian immortality has never shone upon the painter's mind. Yet restricted as is the sphere of æsthetic suggestiveness in Buddhist countries, the world of nature is the same in the east as in the west. Human life has abundant variety and may furnish without limit interesting subjects to the artist working in China and Japan. Flower forms grow spontaneously and with much independence, as if they will not be restricted, whatever the gardener may do to control them by the fashions of an age. The native artists of these countries for a thousand years or more have studied flowers and drawn them with Chinese ink or with colours, and probably their productions may be quite safely brought into comparison with the flower painting of Holland and other European countries. Here perspective does not affect the question; but when landscape enters, the eastern painters lose in the comparison. As a compensation, however, for the want of perspective, they have acquired the habit of writing with the Chinese brush with the hand resting upon the wrist only. This gives the artist the advantage of being able to make beautiful curves with enviable facility. The grace, beauty and energy of curved lines made with the Chinese brush by those accustomed to use it in writing from boyhood, are the special appanage of Chinese and Japanese art. This is perhaps the chief element of power which now enables the artists of these countries to take a not undistinguished place in the art exhibitions of the west. But to this must be added the decorative insight revealed at the competitive exhibition in Paris.

Mr. Josiah Conder has lately written a paper on the Theory of Japanese Flower Arrangements, in which he shews that the Buddhist custom of offering flowers in the temples of Shakyamuni and Kwanyin has led to the development of a peculiar art known to prevail only in Japan. In accordance with the custom of that country there is the principle of centrality and that of divergence. The flowers may be arranged round an upright stem, or they may follow it as it bends wilfully to the one side or the other. The vases and baskets in which flowers may be placed vary in form and they may be disposed in relation to each other according to rules of art. The Japanese have for centuries practised this art and it is still flourishing among them. It is a curious fact that a Chinese basket maker and his daughter many hundred years ago are mentioned as having furnished a Daimio with certain basket shapes which have since become highly fashionable. Mr. Conder's paper is richly illustrated with woodcuts and it is printed in the transactions of the Asiatic Society of Japan for October, 1889. In Mr. Anderson's works on the Pictorial Art of Japan and that of Professor Rein on the Industries of Japan there is a full recognition of the part that China took in the origination and diffusion of art in Corea and Japan. These authors are, however, too decided in their condemnation of the Chinese art of the present time. · They say it is an utter ruin. Nothing is left of aspiration or achievement. This is certainly a noticeable exaggeration. The fact is that the province of Kiangsu holds just now a high place in calligraphy and in painting. In several of the cities of the Soochow plain there are living or lately deceased artists whose productions have won for them an almost national fame. When decorative pictures are needed to ornament expensive buildings in other provinces it is to this province that orders are sent, because the artists of this locality are specially gifted with originality and skill. It need not then be asserted that Chinese art is dead.

Yet it is indubitable that the modern Japanese school to which it gave origin in the Tang dynasty has now gone for ahead of it in the race of excellence.

CHANGE IN THE CHINESE CLIMATE.

THE climate of Asia is becoming colder than it formerly was, and its tropical animals and plants are retreating southward at a slow rate. This is true of China and it is also the case in Western Asia. With regard to tropical animals in Europe it will be remembered that the lion formerly inhabited Thrace. The elephant in a wild state was hunted by Tiglath Pileser, King of Assyria, near Carchemish which lay near the Euphrates in Syria. This was in the eighth century before Christ. Four or five centuries before this Thothmes III, king of Egypt, hunted the same animal near Aleppo. The region on the right bank of the Euphrates now belonging to the pachalic of Aleppo must at that time have been warmer than now. Formerly when China was well wooded, and the people few in number, wild animals would abound. This explains the fact that in high antiquity the elephant and rhinoceros were known to the Chinese, that they had names for them, and that their tusks and horns wore valued by them. When two centuries before the Christian era they conquered Cochin-China and Cambodia the name of the prefecture most to the south, that is to say, where Saigon now is, was "the Elephant prefecture" and afterwards "Elephant forest." South China has a very warm climate which melts insensibly into that of Cochin-China so that the animals of the Indo-Chinese Peninsula would, if there has been a secular cooling of climate, retreat gradually to the south. This is just what seems to have taken place. For some centuries past elephants have been occasionally sent as presents by the King of Cochin-China to Peking to supply the emperor with the most noble kind of draught animals. For

the worship of the Temple of Heaven they have been repeatedly used. But it is too cold in Peking, where the latitude is 40 degrees north, for the animal to enjoy good health and adapt himself to his duties. The keeper cannot venture to pronounce any of them suitable for the office if they shew the least remainder of their wildness. Years have passed since an emperor has gone to the Temple of Heaven drawn by an elephant. Instead of this he has been conveyed there in a sedan on the shoulders of the ordinary sixteen bearers. Now Jerusalem is about the latitude of Shanghai, and Aleppo and ancient Carchemish are in the latitude of Shantung and Honan. We find in the history of Tso Ch'iu Ming that in the time of Confucius elephants were in use for the army at Chingchou between Ichang and Hankow on the Yangtze river. The latitude of this place is very little south of Shanghai. The passage reads (Legge p. 756) "the king to keep back the army of Woo made the men lead elephants with torches tied to their tails so as to rush upon the troops of Woo." A hundred and fifty years after this we find Mencius speaking of the tiger, the leopard, the rhinoceros, and the elephant, as having been in many parts of the empire driven away from the neighbourhood of the Chinese inhabitants by the founders of the Chou dynasty and previously by the Emperors Yao and Shun. Tigers and leopards have been diminishing in numbers ever since, but they are not yet by any means extinct in China. The elephant and rhinoceros are again spoken of in the first century of our era. Wang-mang, the usurper, trained his troops to boldness by sending them to hunt for wild beasts and for these among the rest. This he did to win favour with the people whose crops greatly suffered from the incursions of hungry animals. Such hunting must have been, however, so far as elephants are concerned, in the extreme south, for the author of the Shwo-wen who wrote in the second century says the elephant is a beast of the southern Yue country by which he would mean Kuangsi and other adjacent parts of South China. The last occasion on which elephants with torches tied to their tails were used to rout enemies in battle appears to have been in the early part of the sixth century when a general of the Liang dynasty adopted this manœuvre. If to these particulars regarding elephants be added the retreat from the rivers of South China of the ferocious alligators that formerly infested them, the change in the fauna of China certainly seems to shew that the climate is much less favourable for tropical animals than it formerly was. In fact it appears to have become dryer and colder than it was. The water buffalo still lives and is an extremely useful domestic animal all along the Yangtze and south of it but is not seen north of the old Yellow River in the province of Kiangsu. The Chinese alligator, a mild species, is found still in the Yangtze but so rare is its appearance that foreign residents in China knew nothing about it till it was described by M. Fauvel. It will probably not survive many years after the 20th century has begun.

The flora is also affected by the increasing coldness of the climate in China. The bamboo is still grown in Peking with the aid of good shelter, moisture and favourable soil, but it is not found naturally growing into forest in North China as was its habit two thousand years ago. It grows now in that part of the empire as a sort of garden plant only, so far as is known at present. It is in Szechuan that the southern flora reaches farthest to the northward. Oranges flourish there under the protection of high mountains and, with the aid of the mild climate there enjoyed. So also the lichee is found there. In the neighbourhood of Shanghai oranges do not grow in the open air, nor can the trees weather the winter unprotected except in the island of Situngting in the great lake near Soochow. In Chêkiang oranges are met with growing in the open air at Wênchow in about 28 degrees of latitude. Western

China is somewhat more tropical in its climate at the same latitude north than is the case with eastern China. The growth of the orange and lichee in Szechuan is an illustration of this fact. The reason is found in the high mountains which in that vast province protect the cultivated plains from the cold winds of the north.

In the selected passages of beautiful writing read all over China under the name of Koo Wen is one by Han Wenkung. He addresses the genius of the alligator and appeals to him as the new prefect of Chaochoufu appointed by the Emperor, to submit to his will and leave the Swatow river if not in three days, then in five, and if not in five then in seven. Go he must, and cease to eat men, oxen, deer, bears, pigs and other animals in that part of the territory marked out of the empire by the great Yü. If he refused, the prefect would select a force of his strongest and most skilful people and pursue him with the strong bow and poisoned arrows till he and all his kindred were exterminated. The alligators obediently disappeared from the Swatow river and were never seen there again. This document was immensely admired and has been highly popular ever since. It dates from the beginning of the ninth century. From it we learn that it was then that the Canton climate became slightly colder than it had been previously, and thus freed the inhabitants from a scourge which they had always suffered from before.

CHINESE VIEWS ON SCIENCE.

THE views now held by intelligent Chinese on the origin of science are that the knowledge possessed by their ancestors leaked out to the men of western nations, who improved on the information they received and gradually developed the sciences and inventions of the modern age. This idea was started by Mei Wu-ngan in the reign of Kanghi and has been maintained ever since with singular persistence. The cultivated class in this country have consoled themselves with this thought during the past two centuries. On the face of this theory there is no small amount of absurdity, but the party of progress know how to make efficient use of it as an argument. The Chinese have been accused of many things. But no one ever yet accused them of want of astuteness in putting reasons in a forcible way, or of not being able to make a good case out of a bad one. This may be exemplified in the use the literary Chinese have made of the result of Mei Wu-ngan's researches into antiquity. Those who are really in favour of introducing foreign improvements say, we wish to make use of the knowledge of western men because we know that what they have attained in science and invention has been through the help that our sages gave them. We have a good right to it. None of our people ought to hinder our getting the full benefit of what is our own. There is a class who are extremely jealous of the intellectual superiority which may be claimed by Europe on account of progress in civilisation. Those who belong to this class say, we will not for a moment allow the claims to superiority. What Europe has done she has done through the help we gave. If we did not exactly give science to Europe we gave them the fruitful germ which produced it. They have the science of optics, but in our Motsz we find that reflection from mirrors was known in the days of Mencius. The men of the west hold that the earth is round. This was believed also by our poet Chü Yuen, who in his ode on astronomy announces this doctrine; and this was not many years after Mencius. This being so we ought not, they add, to be ashamed of the study of western science. We are the rivals of the western kingdoms and it is good policy to use their spears in order to pierce their shields. We ought to train our youth in western science so that we may know how best to meet the men of the west in the struggle to resist their encroachments.

By arguing in this way the Chinese shew that according to their way of thinking political autonomy and national independence are closely linked with the claim of intellectual equality. Political necessity drives them to adopt a certain arrogance of tone which the facts do not justify. If they were politically strong they could do as the Romans did with Greece. The Romans governed Greece and cheerfully admitted that the country they had conquered was the mother of philosophy, science and art. They made no claim to equality with Greece in scientific inventiveness but sent their sons to Athens as to a university. The Chinese are stronger now than they ever were, but they are not strong enough to be able to resign the claim to intellectual equality.

Mei Wu-ngan and others read the books translated by the Jesuits, including Euclid and the teaching of astronomy, and they were delighted with the new views. The Jesuits, however, were in high favour at Court and while they basked in sunshine the native mathematicians shivered in the shade. This was not agreeable and the native astronomers went home each day from Court dissatisfied. Yang Kwang-hsien particularly took a bold stand. He ventured to foretell an eclipse. Adam Schaal foretold the same eclipse and his hours, minutes, and seconds, agreed with the reality. This was a crucial case. All Peking was waiting with interest to know the result. The prophecy of the foreigner proved by its fulfilment the errors of the Chinese mathematician who retired in disgrace from the position which he held. He went back to his home in Hweichou to write the book called "The Inevitable Exposure," which consisted of a series of calumnious and grossly untrue accusations against the Jesuit fathers. This bad book made him much more notorious than did his works on mathematics. The unscrupulous enemies of the western men and of their religion have reprinted this book again and again. At the present time they still do so. But a more intelligent and fair-minded class are ashamed of the book and would burn every copy if they could. Very different was the tone of Mei Wu-ngan who was invited three days in succession by the Emperor (Kanghi) Shengtsu to converse with him for a long time upon mathematical subjects. His attitude was patriotic and scholarly. He had a fondness for mathematics and read voraciously. He was therefore in a position to criticise western knowledge in an appreciative manner. He says of the precession of the equinoxes that the western astronomy explains it not as a slow movement of the ecliptic but of the stars in the sky, while Chinese astronomy has always held it to be a slow motion of the ecliptic. He rejects the Chinese view, which dates from the fifth century, but was wrong in doing so for it was in fact more rational than the other. Sir Isaac Newton, who was the first to explain the precession of the equinoxes, was living at the time, and he taught that the apparent displacement of the stars known as the precession is due to a twist in the earth's axis of revolution, making its north and south poles revolve round the poles of the ecliptic in 25,000 years. This new view condemns both that of the Jesuits and that of the Chinese, for neither do the stars move fifty seconds in a year nor does the ecliptic move that distance. But of the two, the Chinese view is certainly more nearly right. The Jesuits, however, were not then allowed to teach the daring doctrines of the new astronomy. This great scholar died without knowing the advantage in argument that belonged to his country's astronomy on this point.

New views on the shape of the earth and the properties of a right-angled triangle were known very early to the Babylonians and Egyptians and first reached China somewhere about eleven hundred years before Christ. They were taught in the schools of China from that time, but only in those where mathema-

tics was studied. The ordinary literati did not know these doctrines. Yet Tseng-tsz, author of the first of the Four Books, knew of the rotundity. Medical writings of the third century before Christ state the rotundity with unfaltering distinctness. Chü Yuen the poet, in undertaking like Lucretius to describe the system of the universe, gives us the Ptolemaic theory of nine heavens, or nine concentric spheres, which involves a belief in the rotundity of the earth. This theory is called Ptolemy's but in fact it was both Babylonian and Egyptian, and, as we now know, Chinese. It was on these undeniable facts that the great scholar Mei, the friend of Kanghi, planted his foot firmly and said science belonged to China before its light shone over Europe. The Europeans received it from us. It was our sages who gave them the knowledge of the rotundity of the earth and the first principles of geometry.

A MUSEUM AT PEKING.

On account of the large influx of students at the examinations in Peking a museum in that city would be of great advantage. Provision for food and lodging on these occasions has to be made for 20,000 or 30,000 strangers for about a month. This shews the capacity of Peking for entertaining. So also the arrival and departure of high officers, civil and military, causes the entrance and exit of thousands of persons every year. This is so much the more the case because of the great roads leading from the metropolis into Manchuria, Corea, Mongolia, Russia and the Turkish province. The Government appointments of officials to the provinces of China proper and correspondence with them involves an enormous amount of travelling to and from Peking. The constant influx of strangers thus caused would render an attractive museum very useful. It is a city, too, where education is favoured and it should be remembered that in Peking there is an unusual number of schools , and colleges which might be brought into occasional relation with the supposed museum. This would be greatly to the advantage of students who are receiving an education on foreign principles.

The best position for the museum would be at the Office for Foreign Affairs, in connection with the College which will ultimately have conceded to it, it is to be hoped, the powers that will constitute it a real Government University. Such an affiliated institution would have the benefit of the superintendence and efficient aid of the President and Professors of the Tung-wên-kuan. It could thus be worked without friction by the same wheels and movements which work the college. With regard to the objects that should be placed in the museum, they should be similar to those found in national museums in Europe and America as well as those found in special museums and in observatories. The Chinese part should embrace the exhibition of archæological specimens, of books, rubbings of inscriptions, local products, commercial samples. There should be a foreign and native department. No one knows how far the inmates of the palace go to visit the Zoological collection of stuffed animals in the west park adjoining the Cathedral. They were stuffed under Père David's superintendence. Several hundred specimens of birds, beasts, and insects are found there, some of them from foreign countries. Many visits must have been paid by occupants of the palace of all grades to see this collection since the Cathedral was acquired for the palace. This collection is not at all likely to be thrown open to the public. Mongol visitors were formerly allowed to visit certain buildings containing many curious things of a Buddhist kind in the northern part of the park on the edge of the lake. The park is now assigned to the empress dowager and no such liberty can in future be allowed. Mongol visitors in winter are extremely fond of sight-seeing. A museum adjoining the government college would

prove interesting to the princes and their suites who come long distances to pay homage at the new year, especially if the emperor should confer on them the privilege of visiting the museum as a mark of imperial favour. The reason why this mode of conferring the entrée to the museum as a mark of favour is here mentioned is the possibility that without the emperor's express permission official persons would not be persuaded to go see it. Many a Peking resident in the rich families would like to go to Tientsin, see a steamer and take a trip on the railway, but cannot venture because "his duties do not call him there." Some plan needs to be carefully excogitated which should ensure the proposed museum being inspected by official persons as such and at the same time prove no bar to the inspection of the museum by non-official persons and by ladies. Vast crowds visit the fairs of Peking and none more than the new year fair for the sale of curios, books, precious stones and pictures. This proves that Peking is inhabited by a population taking great pleasure in sight-seeing.

The native archæologists of China have for several centuries done much useful work and during the present dynasty they have shown great activity. Every antique cash, vase, mirror, foot rule, musical instrument or inscription has been studied and written about with ingenious elaboration. It is time that there should be a museum in Peking accessible to students who wish to examine antiques or copies of antiques. The stone drums are already there and there is no bar to observing them. The Confucian temple where they are kept was built in the time of the Mongol sovereignty of China. They were brought there from Honan, where they were kept for several centuries while the capital was in that province. They are now in the *gateway* of the temple, so that the great scholars of the country seem not to have known exactly what best to do with these relics. They should not be removed, for they are well under cover and are not likely to be injured by weather. But other such relics should, when found, be provided with a refuge in the museum. It was not long ago that a considerable collection of coins of the Roman Emperors was discovered. Money minted in Europe in the first and second centuries found its way to China and was there recently recovered. It is a pity that these coins should not be retained in China in a public museum, because Europe has numberless Roman coins and can very well do without these. They ought to be purchased for a museum in Peking, and in the catalogue of such a museum the circumstances of their discovery in Shansi should be related and their similarity to coins in European museums pointed out. Such a catalogue in Chinese would be a very saleable book, because there are archæologists in every province and prefecture. Admission to the museum should be free and a profit made by the sale of catalogues. The catalogues should be prepared by the professors, each taking charge of his own department. There would be an international and legal chamber, a chamber for natural philosophy, astronomy and chemistry, for physiology and anatomy, for zoology and botany, for the products of England, France, America, Germany, Russia, Africa, India, and other countries. Such a museum would not only gratify the sight-seer, but would have a most important educational influence on the country.

◆

THE MIGRATION OF INDUSTRIES.

THE inevitable result of the gradual change taking place in the Chinese climate is the migration of industries from North to South. This is true for example of varnish and silk, which in the most ancient times were products of North China as the valuable geographical record, the Yü Kung, tells us. These articles so characteristic of China and so useful in promoting the industry and civilisation, and thereby the wealth

and population of the country, are spoken of together in that treatise as tribute from Shantung four thousand years ago. The varnish tree is mentioned also in the Book of Odes in a poem located in Weihwei Fu, now belonging to north-eastern Honan. Though the produce of the tree is not mentioned there, yet the fact that that part of China has the same latitude as Shantung, renders the fact a valuable one. Also one of the tributaries of the Wei in north-western China was called the Varnish River, and the resident population civilised by the Chow imperial family about B.C. 1200 had partly come from the neighbourhood of this river. The name would naturally originate, if not bestowed on account of the dark colour of the channel or the banks, from the trees that grew near it. At present the varnish tree grows in Szechuan, in Kueichow, and to a small extent on the hills of Ningpo. A large part of the varnish which pays duty at the foreign custom houses finds its way to Hankow from the south and west and there becomes distributed, eight thousand piculs leaving Hankow each year. Shanghai distributes 3,000 piculs of varnish in a year through the foreign customs. The lacquer ware of Ningpo has a good repute and here 1,100 piculs of varnish are imported yearly. This is an instance of the migration of industry. The lacquer ware of China which is the parent of the lacquer ware of Japan, would be first made in the northern provinces, when varnish was produced there. Now however the lacquer ware industry flourishes in central and southern China chiefly. South China receives a good portion of its varnish from Saigon and Cochin China. As this tree formerly produced varnish in thirty-six degrees of latitude and now produces it in the belt of country south of about 32 degrees, we may suppose that Shantung four thousand years ago had as mild a winter as Shanghai has now, and the Yellow River would not be frozen over perhaps in any part of it course.

In regard to the silk industry it should be noted that the merchants who in the times of the Roman Empire engaged in the silk trade as then conducted by the Central Asian route, in taking with them silk manufactured into cloth, would naturally take that of north China. North China has ever since the earliest mention of silk in the Yü Kung, continued to produce silk, and there is no province where the mulberry tree and the silkworm are not found, but with the cooling of the climate the main production of silk has come to belong to the central provinces ; so that last year Shanghai exported 116,000 piculs. Wuhu and Hankow produced, for export 1,800 and 21,000 piculs respectively. Ichang exported 11,000 piculs. Thus in the Yangtze valley 150,000 piculs were exported, while from Canton, Kowloon and Lappa the amount was not much more than a fourth of that, or 40,000 piculs of silk. Chefoo exported 14,000 piculs and Newchwang of oak leaf silk 13,000 piculs. This is the result now after more than 4,000 years of the cultivation of the mulberry and the silk worm oak and the production of silk. The proportion of silk culture in north China then is now one fifteenth of that of all China. Three-fourths•of the whole export is from central China and to make up the remaining fourth Canton sends away three times as much as Chefoo. The conclusion to be drawn from these facts is, that north China is becoming gradually less suitable than it was for the mulberry tree and the silkworm, which prefer a warmer temperature than they now find there. The Governors of the Southern provinces may well aim at an extension of the silk culture in their jurisdiction. This they are now doing. Among the latent causes which lead them to this action is in reality this one, the gradual cooling of the climate. The origin of the silk culture of central China must be dated about B.C. 1200 when the Chow family sent out a colony to Soochow. The Chow family would teach the aborigines on the banks of the

Yangtze agriculture, house building and weaving. At least we know by the Book of Odes that they did this in the upper valley of the Wei in Shensi a little earlier. What they did—for the aborigines in Shensi in shewing them how to build suitable houses they would do in the Soochow plain in introducing silk weaving. The silkworm is native to the north and feeds on oak leaves as well as on leaves of other trees. In central China the mulberry is planted purposely and the silk industry in all its departments may safely be regarded as introduced from another locality. The Soochow plain was the appanage of a great colony settled in the Shang dynasty and governed by members of the Chow imperial family. The colonies of the ancient Chinese were led by men who taught both useful arts and good morality. It was in this way that the foundations were laid of the great homogeneous nation which we now see occupying China Proper. Unity was produced by uniformity in instruction. No outside races were prevented from absorption, but while they were absorbed they became the possessors of a like industry and morality with the race which absorbed them. We see how the system works at Newchwang. On account of quick growth of population in Shantung the Manchurian province was colonised. Many Shantung people went there by junk from Chefoo. They introduced the industries with which they were familiar. This was the origin of silk manufacture there. The *Quercus Sinensis* grew wild and the cocoons which were found on it were capable of being utilised by the new emigrants. About twenty years ago the silk of the oak leaf silkworm began to be exported from Newchwang, to meet a demand by the manufacturers of plush and velvet. The natives of Shantung were well able to extend the production in Manchuria, because they were thoroughly accustomed to this culture in their own country. Their success shews that oak silkworms in forty degrees of latitude do well, but probably produce a finer silk in latitude thirty-six. Mulberry fed worms do fairly well in latitude thirty-six, but thirty-one suits them better, while on the left bank of the West river in Canton province in twenty-three degrees they also do remarkably well. There is a good demand in Europe for Canton silk which is produced in twenty-three degrees of latitude. The planting of the silk industry in eastern Canton ought to be a success as also in Kuangsi and Kueichow. The Chinese high officials who are seeking to spread sericulture in those parts of the country are to be commended for the effort, which it may be expected will result in making the people richer and increasing the revenue of the empire. The mulberry tree silk was formerly produced in latitude thirty-six with a minimum temperature of twenty-five in the winter. The industry migrated southward when the winter minimum sank to ten in the north and the Yangtze valley acquired the trade which earlier was enjoyed by the population that lined the Yellow River.

CHINA'S TURKISH PROVINCE.

SINCE the Chinese government extinguished the internal rebellions which caused such widespread anarchy in the reign of Hsien Fêng, its policy has been to extend the number of provinces and change military for civil government wherever it was possible. This has been done in Chinese Turkestan and in the Moukden province. In doing this, the object has been not to introduce a new system but to expand the area of the existing civil administration. The military commandant of Moukden was changed for a civil governor. So also Sin Keang, when conquered by Tso Tsung-tang, was reduced to a province to be ruled on the same principles as China proper. The Mahommedan rebellion there was crushed and Chinese rule re-established on a more secure basis than before. The Turkish and Persian Mahommedans cannot be permitted to separate themselves from Chinese control within the Chinese

territory, any more than autonomy could be allowed to the Mahommedans in India or in Russia. The advantage of appointing a governor is found in his being able to control the civil officers of each city as well as those who are military. Immediately under him are, the brigadier-general (chen t'ai) who has the troops in his care, and the taotais, who govern the city magistrates. After the successive attacks made in Formosa by the Japanese and the French, the Foochow governor was transferred to Formosa in order that there might be in the island a central authority who could decide matters of doubt, and act with promptitude in emergencies. This step was not taken till after it had been long thought about. Political events hastened it after the accumulation during some years of documents sent to Peking to point out its advantages. The extension of this system of civil administration in Tartary, both in the Turkish and Manchu provinces, is likely to prove quite successful because of the increase of emigration from China proper in these two regions. The fecundity of the Chinese race in all parts of China proper has been specially remarkable during the last two centuries, and as droughts and floods have never been more destructive than they are now, emigration becomes inevitable. This renders it a necessity to extend into the agricultural tracts of Tartary the civil administration to which the emigrants were accustomed in their original homes. A Chinese writer says that western maps are defective when they come to those parts of Asia which are not accessible by sea and are seldom visited by travellers. Once, however, he tells us, when he was in Calcutta he looked at one map in a museum which gave very minute details of the Chinese possessions in central Asia. He copied it and translated the names of places, rivers and mountains into Chinese. On returning to his own country he compared his map with Chinese maps made in successive periods and with the information given in Chinese history, adding more minute particulars found in books of the present dynasty. He inserted boundaries, telegraph lines, railways and other novelties in the Russian portion, marking them with appropriate colours for greater distinctness. He made his map, he says, so that the T'sung-ling chain, between Russian Turkestan on the west and that of China on the east, was just in the middle. This chain he describes as dividing from each other the three great empires of Asia. The mountain mass of which it is composed is very lofty, full of windings, and extremely precipitous. It is a sort of first ancestor of all the mountains of the continent. On the east is Chinese Turkestan and Tibet, on the south are the possessions of England in India. On the west and north are the Russian provinces. The T'sung-ling chain has been known to China for two thousand years and has frequently been made the western frontier of the empire. Many have been the vicissitudes in the government of the territory lately made into a new province by the Peking administration. First there were thirty-six kingdoms. These were afterwards increased to fifty. Probably at that time we may suppose that the inhabited oases in the new province were wider than now and more numerous. Desert sands tend to spread with the lapse of time. The pomegranate and vine have apparently disappeared recently from Hami, where they were a thousand years ago a very prominent object, as we learn by comparing Hiuen Chwang's travels and those of Fa-hien with modern Russian accounts. One of the chief peculiarities in the Sinkeang province, as it is now termed, has been the change of religions. Before Buddhism there was the religion of the old Turkish stock, mixed with Persian elements. This was changed for a Hindoo religion, because a northern race conquered northwestern India. Buddhism spread monasteries over the oases of that country and they remained there from the second to the eighth century, when

Mahommedanism drove out Buddhism by its superior vigour. The Turkish population submitted to the brighter intellectual force of the Persians, who had then become devout Mahommedans. The Mahommedan religion has been there now for a thousand years. It would gladly have founded a government of its own, but lacks the force to be derived from the foreign weapons of attack and foreign drill which the Chinese now have. Tso Tsung-tang's campaign overthrew Mahommedan hopes of autonomy, and made it possible for our Chinese author to imagine himself on the summit of the T'sung-ling chain in the centre of the world, looking out on the three empires of China, England and Russia where they meet. For several centuries also the Nestorian missions spread Christianity in parts of Sinkeang. Prester John was a king somewhere in that country, or rather near it, who favoured Christianity and whose daughter was a Christian. Christianity was a somewhat weak power in those parts for six centuries till it was overwhelmed by Tibetan Buddhism when reinvigorated by the celebrated Tsungkaba. All through these ages China was large enough for the Chinese, and their merchants in the silk trade simply came and went along the northern and southern roads of Sinkeang. But China is now, notwithstanding her misfortunes, in a new era of prosperity, characterised by rapid growth in the population as its most striking feature. Under the new *régime* all the space available for agriculture in the oases of the Sinkeang plains ought naturally to be filled by Chinese emigrants flying from those droughts and floods which hopelessly beset them in their own country. Sudden poverty, the loss of harvest, the destruction of homes, poor at the best, by an unexpected deluge, all compel emigration, and when the new province is filled by the fugitives, Russia might well open her arms to receive the overflow and provide them with lands to cultivate and flocks to tend.

MEDICINE IN CHINA.

THE gift of healing tends powerfully in modern times to promote the unity and brotherhood of mankind. Medical missions form a prominent part of the modern missionary enterprise; and this connection will be in the future more and more developed because medical knowledge and skill readily become self-propagating. Few persons are aware how extensively vaccination is practised in China by native operators, who learned the art in the first instance at Canton almost at the beginning of this century. At that time a surgeon on the staff of the East India Company, under the impulse of philanthropy introduced the practice of vaccination ,and it has been spreading in the country ever since. This gift to China has already proved of immense value, and the incidental cause of its diffusion is found in the rotatory nature of the mandarinate, which takes officers of intelligence to Canton, for instance, for a time, and then transfers them after a few years' residence to some other part of the country. Magistrates are removed from city to city, and this has aided in the propagation of Western improvements which in the old days entered China at Canton exclusively. The practice of vaccination in Peking is known to have commenced in this way, and from that city it has extended and is still extending through the eleven prefectures of the province. At the meeting of the Missionary Conference at Shanghai in 1890 it was mentioned that the rapid sale of morphia pills has fixed the attention of medical missionaries at the present time as an evil to be deplored, and their earnest advice was tendered to the missionary body to discourage it firmly among the Christians. A remarkable feature in the missions at present is the increased number of medical men, of whom no fewer than twenty were present at the Conference. The excellent works prepared by Dr. Hobson in Chinese on medical subjects thirty years ago are still on sale, and these books have been extremely useful in opening the way to the knowledge of the Western art of healing for Chinese readers. How many valuable works of others, such as Drs. Kerr, Dudgeon, Porter, Osgood, and Douthwaite have been more recently produced the book lists show. The amount of knowledge, not only strictly medical, but dietary, sanitary and scientific thus communicated to the Chinese has been very great, and this is all recognised by the missionaries generally and by the societies who send them out as an essential part of the enterprise to which they are committed. Contemplating medical missions from another very important point of view, missionaries who heal the ailments of the Chinese are the representatives of the whole medical profession of Europe and America, a body essentially philanthropic, and are engaged in introducing as rapidly as it is possible to do every beneficial feature in the healing art as now practised in the West.

Medicine in China is very old. In the year 579 before Christ cure by the moxa and acupuncture were already practised by Chinese physicians, for it is in that year that this treatment is first mentioned in any book, Chinese or foreign. The passage will be found in page 374 of Legge's Chinese classics, volume fifth. In addition to this there was the celebrated Pien-tsio, who some time during the period from the eighth century before Christ to the sixth performed remarkable cures by feeling the pulse first and basing his treatment upon the indications. On one occasion he was in attendance on a prince who was in a state of unconsciousness for five days, and he depended on pulse feeling for his knowledge of the patient's condition. He was probably a native of Hochienfu in Chihli. The stories told cannot all have been true of him as an individual, belonging as they do to different centuries. They indicate, however, that the feeling of the pulse was in use among physicians at that early time. Hippocrates, the founder of Greek medicine, certainly lived in the sixth century, and in his time the pulse had already become the fulcrum of Chinese medical practice. The knowledge of this fact helps in fixing a limit for the field of investigation into the healing art of China. The history of that art spreads over six centuries before Christ, and nineteen centuries afterwards. Medicine flourished when literature and philosophy flourished. The great books of Chinese medicine, the *Soo wén* and the *Ling ch'oo*, were written at about the same time as the Four Books or a little later. Thus they belonged to the age of the sages. They mark the first prosperous period of this noble art, when it had escaped from the hands of exorcists and diviners who in earlier ages had been accustomed to care for the sick. They are the classics of Chinese medicine and in them its theory and principles are enshrined. In these books we find such statements as that metal and water combine, in accord with the influence of Venus and Mercury. The soul is spoken of as something distinct from though included in the body. Madness, fever, apoplexy, paralysis, cholera, are here all described. The five elements are represented as revolving powers and, they correspond to the five planets in the heavens. The earth moves westward through space which surrounds it below as well as above and around. Ignorance of astrology is stated to be a cause of disease and death. Interlaced with the doctrine of the five elements is found the doctrine of the dual principles of darkness and light each divided into greater and lesser. The veins and arteries are here described as canals originating in the skin which consequently is that part at which all disease commences its invasion on the human frame. The possibility of the human subject securing immortality by Taoist methods is discussed and the affirmative is believed. The *Soo wén* having in it these and other curious things, such as the rotundity of the earth and the doctrine of a universal and primæval vapour, and having as already said a distinct tincture of the Mesopotamian astrology, constitutes in itself a convincing proof that China was receptive of Western knowledge to a large extent in the fifth, fourth, and third centuries before Christ. From that time during more than two thousand years China has been under the dominion of the philosophy of this book. She has been so through the whole range of native medical thought. The composition of new medical books has never ceased during that long continued time. Among these works the *Pen-ts'au*, the *Materia medica* of the Ming dynasty, is the most useful and comprehensive.

It stands to reason that Chinese medicine deserves to be studied, and a fuller account of it than we yet have ought to be given in the English tongue. The number of physicians now embraced in the missionary circle is so great that there is hope that some one of them will become the historian of Chinese medicine, by preparing a careful narrative of its growth and present state, and thus do what Sprengel has done for the history of medicine in Europe. It may be confidently predicted that such a work would shew that Chinese medicine, being the result of the uninterrupted experience of two thousand five hundred years, in spite of its Babylonian theory, now exploded by modern discoveries, is deserving of high respect for its practical utility in many important ways.

CHANGES IN THE AGRICULTURE OF NORTH-CHINA.

IN the province of Chihli maize has become a common product during the last half century. The grains are large and very nutritive and the stalks useful for fuel. The cost of living when maize meal is used is much less than for wheat flour. In a climate which is so cold in winter as that of the province of Chihli wheat flour is a very favourite article of food and is felt to be more satisfying than others. The well-to-do like it on this account. If the population of Chihli were appealed to as to what cereal suited them best for daily food they would by a large majority vote for wheat flour. The rich, however, being able to purchase animal food have rice daily. Rice is stored in the granaries, and distributed to the bannermen for themselves and their families. These families use the cheaper kinds, but sell the dearer. If poor, they live on maize meal chiefly as being cheaper than other sorts of food. Maize has spread from western Asia into China during the present dynasty. Excellent rice is produced on river banks in favourable positions and always commands a good price. Such favourable positions are however few. The chief product is small millet for human food and Barbadoes millet for animals. Small millet which is used as bird seed in Europe is now perhaps the chief food of man in the northern provinces. But was this always so? Probably the recent application of the word *ku*, formerly meaning all kinds of grain, to signify ordinary millet is an index to the fact that anciently the ordinary food was not millet and that there has been a change. The northern people when they gradually came to adopt this kind of small millet as their staple article of food, at the same time as if by unconscious general agreement united to call it by this name. So also wheat is corn in England and maize is corn in the United States.

The oldest quotation in the Chinese Classics mentioning the five elements, water, fire, metal, wood, and earth, adds a sixth "grain." These were early singled out as the six classes into which the governor of the country could conveniently distribute the objects coming under executive control. But grain did not remain in the classification long. The five elements of China and of Persia were after this time regarded as complete without a sixth. The grain sown in various localities came soon to be spoken of as the "hundred grains" or "the five grains." Among the five, rice stood first. They were rice, hemp, millet, wheat, beans. Now wheat as we know was then grown in mountainous regions and ancient writers tell us that

rice and pulse were the food common in the plains. To these we must add millet and panicled millet. Thus we have in view the five grains of China twenty-five centuries ago. In the time of Confucius the tall millet also, reaching ten feet high, was grown for the food of animals as it is now everywhere in north China.

Wheat and oats bear cold weather best, and oats grow in a colder climate than wheat. At present wheat is produced abundantly in Kiangsu but it gives the best flour in Shantung and the climate of that province is probably the most suitable for wheat of any in China. Oats grow as far south as Yünnan because of the height, from four to six thousand feet, of the plateau of the province above the sea. It is a highland grain by preference and will also grow on low grounds where there is a moist cold winter. It is modern like maize and potatoes in China, and on account of the stimulus applied to its cultivation by the growth of population it is on the ascending grade. Oats, potatoes, and maize are employed as food just now more than ever in north and west China for the three reasons, that the isothermal lines are, as compared with two thousand years ago, retreating towards the south, that commerce has brought these productions recently to China by the central Asian route, and that in a nation with a growing population domestic economy requires this change in food to counterbalance the increasing poverty. Potatoes for example are spreading in highland China with unexampled rapidity, just as they did in Ireland at a time when the people of that island grew in a few decades from two or three millions to eight millions, and the relief of emigration was required to reduce the too great pressure on the means of subsistence. Over a great part of north China now, wheat and rice are the food of the well-to-do. Autumn and spring wheat are both produced extensively. Rice is grown once in the year in the warm summer where rivers favour irrigation, and there is no better rice than that cultivated a few miles from Peking on the west where the Hwun Ho issues from the mountains, and has during myriads of years scooped out a valley of its own which now possesses a few alluvial tracts supplying excellent white rice for the wealthy families of Peking. But the great rice-growing region is not here. It is in central China, on the Yangtze River, that rice is grown for export on a large scale.. The reason is that the heat of the climate there is just sufficient to suit this product. In 1888 from the port of Shanghai four million and a half piculs of rice were shipped to the northern and southern provinces. In 1887, the quantity shipped was 3,800,000 piculs. Last year on account of floods and a prohibition to export, except under special permit, the quantity sank to less than 2,000,000 piculs. Most of this large export reaches Shanghai from rice growing grounds up the river, the land near Shanghai being pre-occupied with cotton and indigo required by the native looms of all the villages in the Shanghai plain. But the main product of the soil from Shanghai west along the great Yangtze valley to Hankow is rice. At Shanghai rice is sown once in the year and the time is May, the harvest being in September. This is in latitude thirty-one. Just a little farther to the South there are two crops of rice in the year. At Ningpo, latitude thirty, rice is sown in April and July and harvested in August and October. Shanghai is thus the centre of the national rice trade and the rice merchants of this port do an enormous business.

Let us compare this state of things with what we know of ancient China. This will help us to decide whether the climate of China is gradually getting colder. In the *Chow li*, a book of the time before Confucius, we have a section upon the products of the different parts of north and central China. There were then in the country thirty-nine tribes of various races ruled by the Chinese. The races to which they belonged were

six who were, we may suppose, Coreans, Turks, Tungus, Tibetans, Burmans, and Shans. We may apply these names because they seem roughly to answer the question " what languages those six races spoke ?" Chinese civilisation taught all these aborigines to plough, sow and weave cloth, and they became by intermarriages a part of the great Chinese nation. The productions of the old nine provinces are briefly mentioned. Rice occurs as a prominent product in all but three of the modern provinces. The exceptions are Shanse, Shensi and Kansu. Thus Shantung produced rice and wheat: Hupeh and Hunan produced rice only. Bird seed millet and panicled millet were then the common grain of the Wei valley in Shensi and of Shansi. In the Peking province these two cereals with rice were the farmer's favourites. In the southern part of the same province the farmer sowed the two millets. In Kiangsu the only cereal was rice. It was quite too warm and low for wheat. The people all wore skins, or silk gowns, or cloth made of hemp and other plants having a suitable fibre. Cotton and indigo had not then been introduced and it was about fifteen centuries after the time we are describing before the Chinese learned to cultivate these productions. Altogether it may be concluded that some cause, such as great height above the sea, prevented the cultivation of rice in the extreme north and northwest corner of the empire, and that elsewhere throughout the country rice was freely grown, aided by the fertilising waters of the Yellow River, especially in Honan and Chihli. The climate therefore must have been warmer then than it now is.

This independent argument from changes in agricultural products for the increasing coldness of the Chinese climate, is to be added to the disappearance of the varnish tree industry and of the greater and better part of the silk industry from the northern provinces. Altogether it seems difficult if not impossible to evade the conclusion that a slow change in climate is proceeding, and that any given isothermal line is now to the south of its former position.

———◆———

CHINESE ACCOUNTS OF THE MAMMOTH.

THE gradual cooling of the Asiatic climate may be supported by the existence of the bones of the mammoth in northern Siberia. This hairy elephant lived in that country when the air was temperate and when abundant forests supplied it with the young twigs on which it lived. Since that time northern Siberia has become an intolerably cold desert. The ground there is constantly frozen to a depth of more than two feet below the surface and produces only moss with a few modest looking flowers. The mammoth very early drew the attention of the Chinese. It is first mentioned in the *Er-ya* and next in Chuang-tse in the third century before Christ. The enormous quantities of valuable ivory which the remains of the mammoth in Siberia furnish made known to the ancient Chinese the existence of the animal through their trade with Tartary. On account of its being found in very many localities imbedded in the soil and in rocks, old books always speak of it as a monstrous mole living underground. It was found, they tell us, in China and in Tartary. Chuang-tse wrote as a poet and pictures it (*yen shu*) as drinking a river of water before its thirst was satisfied. He had been told of the fossil bones or seen them and filled up the picture by the aid of imagination either his own or that of those from whom he heard the story. Seven centuries afterwards a medical writer, Tao Hung-king, says "it is found in forests, and is as large as a water buffalo. It is 'in form something like a pig. Its colour is a greyish red, its feet are like those of the elephant. Its breast and upper tail are white, and blunt though powerful. Its flesh is eaten and is like that of the cow. It is known by the name "King of the Shu tribe. In calamitous years this animal often appears."

In the seventh century this account of the animal was discredited. Its great size was not believed. Its hiding and walking in the earth were thought absurd. These disparaging criticisms were made by Chên T'sang-chi, an eminent writer, who does not seem to have been shewn any of the bones of the animal. Yet in the 11th century Su Sung defended the statements of early writers on this subject. Bones of some large unknown animal had been found at T'sangchou near Tientsin, just as the *Tsin* History states that at Sinencheng, a little way south-west of Nanking, there had been found similar remains in the third century. It was also related that the same animal existed in Tartary where the larger specimens weighed 1,000 catties and was fond of living in water. It was like an elephant in the legs though it had the hoofs of a donkey. Another place where it was found was at Tsihning near Pingyang Fu in Shansi. The people called it the "recumbent cow." It used to wander among the mountains at times and drop its hair in the fields. Each one became a rat and great was the consequent damage to the crops. The Liang history says that in Japan there is a large animal like a cow of the Shu class which is eaten by a great serpent. These are all instances of the mammoth *yin shu* (*yin* "hidden,") and prove the correctness of Tao's words. Tao has been blamed without reason by men who had not themselves inquired into the truth of his statements. The name by which this animal is known in Shensi is "the small donkey." Such are the testimonies of the existence of the mammoth collected by the author of the *Pent'sao*. The Chinese accounts of a monster animal as given in the *Pent'sao* could not if taken alone be regarded as agreeing with the Siberian mammoth except in a rough way, yet they are very important. Early in this century the remains of that animal were found in so many parts of Siberia and the ivory was of such great commercial value that the whole scientific world was interested. Cuvier in France was absorbed in the contemplation of the remarkable bones submitted to him and decided that as the mammoth was met with often with the flesh undecayed, there must have been a sudden change of climate from temperate to extremely cold to account for the frozen condition in which the remains were found. Klaproth who was then at Kiachta visited the Chinese drug shops and found that the bones were known to the Chinese there. They gave him the name of the animal as it was recorded in the *Pents'ao*. It was he that suggested that the throne of ivory of the Mongol Emperors was formed of the tusks and teeth of the Siberian mammoth and that Chinese traders for two thousand years would be ready to buy on any occasion the ivory which was from time to time discovered and brought away. He went home to Berlin and made known to the learned world that the Chinese had accounts of the animal. The passages he translated are apparently those which are found in the *Pents'ao* in the chapter on the class *Shu* which includes the *Rodentia* with the squirrel, sable, ermine, and weasel. There can be no doubt that the mammoth and possibly other fossil animals known to the Chinese are assigned to the class *Shu*, because they were supposed to hide themselves in the soil of cultivated fields and to have died underground in the position where their bones were afterwards found.

In a work published in 1887, "The Mammoth and the Flood," by Henry Howorth, M.P., author of a History of the Mongols, the attempt is made to prove that the change of the Siberian climate from mild to severe was sudden. Lyell's uniformitarian doctrine is opposed. Yet the evidence from China of a gradual change of climate in that country was not known to this author, and if he had had this evidence before him shewing as it does that there is a very slow refrigeration taking place, causing gradual changes in the vegetable as well as the

animal world, he might have modified his theory. Perhaps the best form for the hypothesis to assume is that of a rapid local refrigeration in Siberia, joined with a slow refrigeration generally over the Asiatic continent. The Chinese facts on climate point distinctly to a slow refrigeration, but do not in any way suggest a sudden catastrophe by which the heat shewn by the thermometer was reduced to a large extent. The Chinese mammoth has been found in four principal localities; in the Yellow River alluvium near Tientsin, in the loess formation near the centre of Shansi, in Shensi, also on the banks of the Yangtze River in Anhui. It was this last discovery that drew the attention of Tau Hung-king, who belonged to Nanking, and being a noted Taoist and a writer of the school of Pao Pu-tsz would feel the deepest interest in the discovery so near his home.

RICE.

THE time when the Grand Canal was made separates the Middle Ages of China from the modern period. Just at that epoch the dryness of the northern climate which had been increasing century after century rendered a great water communication necessary to link the north and south together, and this could only be effected by a powerful dynasty like that of the Mongols, which for the first and only time in all history, combined Persia, Russia, Siberia and China in one empire. The Mongols had no civilisation of their own, but they had an instinct for accomplishing great things and they had faith in themselves and in their destiny, a faith which gave them political energy. They believed themselves to be visibly aided by the Providence of the Eternal Heaven. This favourite and energetic expression was then their word for God. The idea of joining Hangchow, the capital of Southern China, with Peking, the capital of Northern China, the one on the thirtieth degree of latitude and the other on the fortieth, pleased the Mongols. It was too early then to change the provincial tribute into silver. It was better to send it in the form of grain, according to the old traditional plan. When the south was conquered the question came up for consideration, how shall the tribute of the south be conveyed? The answer was, by the construction of a great canal. Silver could not then be found in sufficient quantity. Grain at that time was as it had always been a sort of national currency. As copper cash was money so also grain in pints, bushels and piculs was money. There was no way of avoiding the necessity then felt for a great canal by which the government might receive its dues and support the metropolitan population of soldiers, civil officers, and traders. This is what the Peking administration just six hundred years ago were thinking about. Their great army of dependents in the two hundred boards and officers of the capital were paid their salaries half in grain and half in paper money. What the cabinet had to do was to amalgamate north and south as best they could. The Cathay of European old geography was North China, which had then been a separate kingdom during a century and a half. The Manji of old geographers was South China also, including Hupeh and Szechuan. This great political achievement of the Yuen dynasty synchronised with the change brought about in agriculture by the increasing dryness of the climate. The time had come when millet, raised by dry agriculture had replaced rice, raised by wet agriculture, all over the north. The Mongols drove out the Golden Tartars from North China and conquered from the Chao imperial family the whole of rice-growing China.

If any one will look into Kang-hi's Dictionary under *tao*, "rice," he will find it stated that the *Yün-hwei*, a dictionary of the Yuen dynasty, remarks of *tao*, that it is the white rice *now cultivated* in the south for the people's ordinary food. This mode of speaking certainly implies that the writer, living six centuries ago, had an impression that a change had taken place in agriculture on a grand scale. In the way that old books speak of rice we see proof that wherever water came down in streams over the northern plain country so as to be suitable for irrigation, rice was grown. But at present the way of speaking is different. The expression found in the dictionary in question of the 13th century is a specimen of it. Then let us also take into consideration and carefully weigh the classical expression *Shih yü hu tao*, "rice is reaped in the tenth month." It is found in the Book of Odes, in that section which contains the local poetry of the Pin duchy in the western part of Shensi, latitude thirty-five. The question is, was rice reaped in November or in September in the valley watered by an affluent of the Wei River, three thousand years ago? The new calendar of Woo Wang was promulgated about B.C. 1120. The months were so altered in the new calendar that November instead of being the tenth month as it was previously, became the eighth month. Chinese native scholars are of opinion that the poetry preserved the old expressions and that it is November, that is meant. In changing the calendar for official use, the old poem would remain unaltered. Even if it was September that was meant or that the text of the poem was changed to suit the new calendar, it still remains to be explained how it was that an ordinary agricultural process of this kind could then take place in north-west China in the latitude of thirty-five degrees, when it suits that of thirty much better. We seem to be driven to the conclusion that the climate in north-west China was both moister and hotter three thousand years ago than it is now. We had better accept the account given by Chinese native scholars of this calendar and in accordance with their judgment relegate the poem in which these words occur to the beginning of the fifteenth century before

Christ, previous to the time of the change of the calendar in the twelfth century. If we do this, and if the document is free from mistakes, we learn that about B.C. 1400 November was the time when near the Yellow River in Shensi rice was harvested, for it was about that time that Kung Lew, the representative of what afterwards became the Chow imperial family, was living in that region.

At present rice cultivation extends from Hankow all the way up the Han river to Hanchung Foo, in the thirty-third degree of latitude. Richthoven when travelling describes the remarkable change in the character of the country when the Ch'inling range is crossed by a traveller southward bound. The loess is left and South China with its rice cultivation is reached at once. This mountain range is the southern boundary in this longitude of the loess agriculture. The whole of the loess region is now devoted to agriculture without irrigation as a rule. Formerly on the other hand rice was cultivated over a large portion of the same tract of country. For example there is evidence of it near Taiyuen Fu in the heart of the loess country. We find in the time of the Three Kingdoms sixteen hundred years ago, that it is casually mentioned that the people there were urged by an able administrator to cultivate rice by irrigation on the banks of a stream called the Water of Longevity. This was intended as an extension of rice cultivation for the production of food in time of drought. The province of Hupeh still retains rice cultivation through its whole extent, and the southern part of Shensi also. This renders the dividing line of the loess and the non-loess country very irregular. It is remarkable that the Golden Tartars should have possessed the loess country almost exclusively while the Sung dynasty possessed the remainder of China. Here we see the operation of Buckle's principle that climate controls history and that the natural features of a country have much to do with the course of public events.

INDUSTRIAL MISSIONS.

INDUSTRIAL missions have done immense good in various countries, and they would certainly be beneficial in modern China. In the early part of this century, Radama, the first King of Madagascar, requested the London Missionary Society to send him artisans. Among those who went were some iron-smelters. From them the Malagasy learned the art of extracting iron from stone, and when after years of persecution the mission was re-established, and the arts of civilisation were extensively taught to the people, it was found that the mode of smelting iron was one of those which had been retained by the natives, all through the long period of persecution and intellectual darkness which had intervened.

Among those who have strongly advocated industrial missions in China was and is Baron von Richthoven, who in his letter on the provinces of Chêkiang and Anhui makes the following remark : " Incalculable benefit might be conferred on China by establishing industrial missions in which practical men would teach the inhabitants improvements in agriculture and industrial pursuits." He represents civilisation as preceding Christianity. But in fact that complex being, man, is on the whole always ready for moral instruction and mechanical occupation contemporaneously. Education trains all the faculties of men, and it should find both moral and physical occupation for the pupil in a school during parts of the same day. Every good school includes in the curriculum a carpenter's shop, horticulture, gymnastics and those muscular exercises called out-door games. The modern educator sees that the whole of human nature is trained to excellence. His eye watches the pupils in every department, to note who is deficient in this or that talent, and he then aims to stir it into activity by special tasks. To suit a boy for his future life his mind, hands, feet, eyes, and ears all go through contemporary training. Western civilisation of the Christian type is now being taught to the Chinese in the missions. They are not by any means instructed in dogma only. The missionary periodicals and translated works on science shew that the Protestant missionary agency is wide in its scope. So also the schools embrace a very wide curriculum. Dr. Mateer, for example, at Tungchow takes his pupils through a twelve years' course; and some very well skilled mathematicians and electricians have left his school after going through the whole of that course of study. Dr. Nevius also has introduced great improvements in fruit culture in Shantung. These instances in the activity of one of the missions shew what a wide scope is embraced in the Protestant missionary propaganda of this century. Such being the mode of development in the evangelical agencies of our time, the proposition to found agricultural and other industrial missions will not be likely to appear strange or unreasonable when brought before the executive Boards of the missions. These Boards are largely composed of laymen engaged in commerce, and they will willingly give their attention to a suggestion of this kind.

Baron von Richthoven during the years 1860 to 1872 visited all the provinces to make geological observations, and at the same time to institute inquiries of a general nature and particularly such as threw light on the prospects of the extension of foreign trade. The thought of industrial missions struck him when in the Fenshui valley to the west of Hangchow. Here a party of western agriculturists might be located. The valley is very rich in semi-tropical vegetation. Forest trees grow luxuriantly, with a dense jungle of shrubbery among which are the most exquisite flowers known in Europe. The gorges are filled with foliage of the most varied kinds. The soil is highly fertile, and yet, when he saw it, was left almost a wilderness. A walk through any part of this region is an experience of the keenest enjoyment. Not far away is

the Kienmushan, on the slopes of which grow large groves of forest trees. The land here was reported to Baron von Richthoven as purchasable at that time for five dollars an English acre. Before the devastation wrought by the Taiping rebels it was worth two hundred dollars an acre. Here one of the Christian industrial missions might be located. Beside grain crops, timber of various kinds could be grown. An immense number of cattle could be reared here and by an industry of this kind a most favourable change could be introduced into Chinese produce. The fertility of this smiling valley would feed thousands of cattle, the value of which would be a large addition to the collected wealth of the neighbourhood, and animal labour to a large extent might be substituted for that of man. An improvement of this kind would be one of the most palpable first successes of such missions, and it would be much appreciated in depopulated districts where cheap animal labour for ploughing, grinding and carrying burdens would be most welcome. In addition to this there would be a proportionate increase in manure for the grain crops, which need it three times during the growth of the plant. This traveller attributes the want of cattle in the valleys of Chêkiang entirely to lack of thought on the part of the Chinese. He would urge on missionary philanthropists that in conducting their operations the improvement of agriculture should be especially kept in view. European methods and foresight are in his view a necessity to transform and improve Chinese agriculture. The rapid growth of vegetation under the hot sun of Chêkiang in its many lovely valleys points to the want of domestic animals; and the addition of these throughout all districts of South China where vegetation now runs to waste is a perfectly feasible enterprise. South China consists of hilly country with a hot sun and a mild winter, while North China consists of alluvial plains with a hot summer and a severe winter. Agricultural missions would. in any valley in South China where vegetation is abundant and land purchasable at a moderate rate, become readily self-supporting. There would be an annual surplus which would easily be made to sustain the ecclesiastical expenditure. In his views on this matter Baron von Richthoven is not likely to be wrong. We all knew how dilatory the Chinese are in initiating a new departure. They suggest a thousand difficulties. They spend great energy in obstruction. They prefer waiting to action whenever any proposed improvement is a novelty. The only thing to be done is for that class of foreigners who will work quietly and loyally to come in and shew them the way. This is the niche which the Protestant missions may fill with an excellent chance of success and obvious benefit to the country at the present time. Of course, when agricultural improvements are fairly commenced, many changes will take place of which no travellers who have visited China have yet thought. Even without the aid of resident foreign agriculturists it is quite phenomenal how widely maize, oats, potatoes, and unhappily the poppy, have dispossessed older familiar crops during the present century.

PAWN BROKERS.

THE character of the Viceroy of Hukuang may be judged of by an act of his which is, although despotic, a move in the right direction as regards the poor. He is a man of strong character who wraps himself in privacy and sees as few visitors as he well can. Such tendencies as his prevent him from being soon understood. His patriotic love for his country, however, was proved at the time of the negotiations with Russia about Ili, and during the French war. That he desires to see the condition of the poor ameliorated is evident from his recent action regarding pawnbroker's interest at Hankow and Wuchang. In conjunction with the Gov-

ernor of Hupeh he has now issued a proclamation to reduce pawnbroker's interest from three and from two and a half per cent. a month to two per cent. This is, in fact, to reduce it from thirty-six and thirty per cent. per annum to twenty-four per cent. Soon after the Viceroy's arrival at the seat of his government he directed his attention to pawnbroking. This he describes as the convenient institution that helps those who are in need. He speaks of it, in fact, as Europeans speak of banking. The people, he says, of Hankow, Hanyang and Wuchang have not yet quite recovered from the three captures by the Taipings of thirty years ago. They are still poor and need money help to surmount difficulties. In these circumstances, the pawnshops provide them with loans; but three per cent. a month is a very large interest to pay, and this has been hitherto the rate charged by some pawnbrokers. More than twenty establishments in Wuchang charge 2½ per cent. and this in China always means per month : the others charge three per cent. This high interest causes great distress to the poorer classes, so as soon as the Viceroy was settled in his new post he moved the Taotai and prefects with the district magistrates to confer with the pawnbrokers on a reduction. This was done and the result is the present system of pawnbrokers' rates, which is to take effect from the first of the sixth month. The Viceroy and Hupei governor claim to have arranged this out of pity for the borrowers and not to have feared to take from the rich and give what was thus taken to the poor. Thirty-five pawnbrokers, one-third south of the river and two-thirds on the north, are stated to have consented to the Viceroy's plan, and will consequently in future never charge more than two per cent. He praises them for their liberality and philanthropy. Such is the mode in which things are done in China; the officials give the order, the capitalists consult and consent, and then the officials praise them for their benevolence.

The Viceroy and Governor proceed to speak of the official loan system which has hitherto been in use. Loans were made at one per cent. a month or at 9/10ths of one per cent. But it is now fixed that government money, at the disposal of the high officials at Wuchang, shall be lent to the people at half of one per cent. a month as a fixed rate. That is to say, that with certain funds lying idle at Wuchang, the high officials will now be content with six per cent. a year as interest from borrowers. The high officials can obtain sufficient guarantees to enable them to do this. It is evident that those who cannot find sureties, that is the very poor, cannot borrow money cheaply at all, and that six per cent. loans can only be obtained by men having local credit, and well to do friends who are willing to be responsible for them.

The special favour shown to the capitalists on this occasion by the Viceroy and Governor is to relieve them for ten years from special contributions to the government service. It will only be after that time that they will be again called on for help to the government. Of course something must be done to reimburse the official loan office for offering to lend at so low a rate as six per cent. per annum, so the loss thus sustained is to be made up from the new native opium receipts fund. This fund, under the care of the Provincial Defence Board, will be able to support the Official Loan Board in doing business on the moderate scale of profit on which the high officials have now decided. In the proclamation the people are told that the funds in the hands of the officials for extraordinary public works or for charity must be guarded from loss in this way. The levy on native opium of twelve cash an ounce here referred to will yield 19,200 cash a picul, or one tael four mace nearly. Hankow and Wuchang require probably at least 7,000 piculs a

year of native opium, and assuming this amount the Defence Board will have 8,000 or 9,000 taels a year from this source. Beside this, opium firms have to pay, as a sort of registration fee on receiving official recognition, the sum of about 300 taels each, and this is also credited to the Defence Board.

Such is the state of things under a vigorous Viceroy in an immense commercial centre like Hankow, at the present time. There appears to be no part of China where the poor can borrow a little money at less than two per cent a month, and the interest is often far above this. Even in Shanghai, where money is plentiful and native bankers will pay on deposits nine per cent per annum, the poor have to pay as a rule two per cent a month in the pawnbrokers shops. Gradually with the extension of foreign intercourse this rate will be regularly lowered, till the poor get their share of the benefits which the rich now enjoy. It is a great calamity if a poor man wishes, in order to support himself and his family, to buy a boat, or a small piece of land, or the goodwill of a shop, or goods to start in a little business, that he should have to pay 24 per cent per annum for the money he borrows. Viceroy Chang is willing to help those who can find good security by allowing them to have small loans at 6 per cent., and other Viceroys will probably follow this good exemple. But it is the increase of intercourse with the western world which alone can bring about a time when the Chinese middle classes shall have better incomes and more of the comforts of life, while the poor shall be able to exchange their miserable homes and their abject surroundings for decent cottages, sufficient food and remunerative occupation.

------❖------

CHINESE VIEWS ON NOVELS.

THE writing of novels began in the thirteenth century and continued to be a favourite occupation of Chinese writers for about three centuries. After this it was felt that enough had been provided, and the production almost ceased. It was principally in North China and under the Tartar dynasties that the tendency began to display itself. It may be regarded as in some way resulting from the introduction of foreign plays, actors and music. Novels were contemporaneous with stage plays, and the composition of romances for singing with foreign music, for reading in a colloquial form, and for acting on the stage was carried on vigorously for about three centuries. The authors concealed their names. The moral teaching of the Confucian school was too powerful for those able men who loved to give rein to their imagination in novel and play writing to be able to venture on publicity. The Confucianists have always been censors keeping watch over morality. It was never with the consent of the always dominant moral philosophers that novels grew to the position of influence they now possess in China.

The censorship of the press exercised by the Confucianists is not at all extinguished at the present time. On July 22nd there appeared in a Chinese newspaper in Shanghai a paper written by an anonymous Confucianist against novels. He writes from Soochow and calls himself a country farmer. He is deeply impressed with the need of continuing the crusade against licentious literature and romances commenced by Chien Kung-yen during the last century, when he founded a school in Soochow for the promotion of healthy study of the classical books. He held that novels are now so prevalent that they amount to a fourth estate in the realm of teaching ; the Confucian, Buddhist, and Taoist literatures being the first, second, and third. But instead of inculcating virtue they lead men into vice. Reading men, farmers, traders, and boys and girls in good families, learn to read them, and those who cannot read hear the story from others who can. It may be questioned whether the moral influence for evil of Chinese works of imagination is, he says, not greater than

that of the books of the three religions for good. They suggest to young men that they should lead a licentious life, and represent killing a man as a noble action. To read of these things produces disastrous results on public morality. The many cases of crime in the courts and the number of those who adopt a robber's career are wondered at by those who do not reflect on the dangerous effect of Chinese novel reading. This author was led to make these observations by the boldness in crime and general immorality of Soochow and its neighbourhood. A very great proportion of this evil state of things is, he thinks, to be attributed to reading books of a bad influence.

This author was followed by Shih ' Cho-tang, who set the example of establishing a paper-burning urn in his family court. Into this urn went unhesitatingly all novels, and every sort of vicious literature on which he could lay hands, and especially the blocks from which they were printed. For these he made wide search in the hope of extinguishing the evil at its source. In order to find money to buy them up, he first used his spare funds and then sold clothing and even his wife's ornaments, in order that the work of destruction might be more complete. After him another helper in the crusade was a conscientious provincial governor who came to Soochow in 1838. His name was Yu Ch'ien. His being first judge and afterwards governor prolonged his connection with Soochow and aided him to watch the effect of his prohibitory proclamations. A fourth name in this series of the champions of morality is Wang Chung-tsêng, prefect of Soochow. He issued proclamations also against vicious pictures. A great effect was observable in the book trade of Soochow. Representatives of sixty-five of the most respectable firms, went together to the city temple, burnt incense and made a vow not to engage in the trade in immoral books. An office was also opened in the Confucian temple of the magistracy for buying up the blocks of all immoral books, including novels, to the number of between 100 and 200 separate works. The criterion adopted was that all printed books, blocks included, which glorify and gild a vicious life and a thief's career ought to be burnt. Not only novels were condemned but also songs of a vicious tendency made more seductive by musical accompaniments. The consequence was an immense combustion of this class of literature in the city of Soochow, so that it became hard to meet with vicious publications. This was, however, nearly half a century ago, and there has been time since for the evil to crop up afresh. After a short time surreptitious editions were cut and copies were once more in extensive circulation. The governor of 25 years ago, T'ing Ji-ch'ang, issued a new proclamation reiterating the order prohibiting immoral publications. At the present time the flood of books of a bad influence is disheartening. Such reading as they furnish has more effect in leading young minds wrong, says the Confucianist censor of morals, than all the influence on the side of right of the teaching of the Sages. He rejoices that the present Treasurer of Soochow, Huang Tsz-chien, is a man who thoroughly sympathises with the crusade which has been led successively by the above mentioned persons during the past century in the city of Soochow.

The foreign reader of Chinese books of an imaginative kind cannot condemn them indiscriminately, because they contain beautiful characters both of men and women, which exhibit an admirable idea of bravery, filial piety, purity of life, loyalty and other noble qualities. But there can be no doubt of the bad influence of many of the native books which familiarise the minds of the young with scenes of vice, and hold up successful crime to sympathetic admiration. It must also be remembered that whatever evil there may be in the actual life of the Chinese, they have among them the firm friends of a high morality. The national conscience and the national literature alike testify with unfaltering voice to the duty of every one to be moral, just, and humane.

THE YANGTZE RIVER.

The Yangtze River flows from Minshan to the sea in a course of about 2,000 miles in length. Chinese accounts do not recognise the claim of the "River of golden sand" to be the true Yangtze. This tributary stream is much larger and longer than the Min, but it is with the Yangtze as with the Missisippi, the smaller stream rules. If a large river like the Missouri comes into another, a smaller one like the Missisippi, at a right angle, it does not on account of its being larger give its name to that other on its way down to the sea. It is a separate river and keeps its proper name. Local usage determines these matters. There is no doubt on Chinese usage in this case for Confucius is reported to have said "the great river has its source in the Min mountain, and there it is as small as a wine cup, but when it reaches Kiangchiu (near Chungking), unless you have a square-built boat and a day without wind you cannot cross it." The Chinese have always been fond of enriching their literature with topographical works ; and one of the oldest of these, the Book of Hills and Seas, describes this river as commencing on two outliers of the Min mountain on its north-east side. This river flows south from the north border of Szechuan for 150 miles till it reaches the Chêngtu plain, known as the garden of China and deservedly called so on account of its marvellous fertility. Thus the river does not pass through any part of Tibet and is entirely a Szechuan river till it leaves Szechuan at the Gorges. This is as Chinese maps trace the river. The Minshan range runs out to the east, gradually takes a south-east direction, and assumes other names while continuing to divide the province from Shensi. The two provinces have a common boundary till Shensi reaches its southernmost point at about fifty miles north of the gorges. The Minshan river and the

Yangtze proper must, taken together, have flowed at this point for nearly a thousand miles through the viceroyalty of the Governor-General of Szechuan. Although the Yangtze is a Szechuan river, flowing first south from 33°latitude to 29° and then north-east through six degrees of longitude to the gorges, it is receiving all the way the rainfall of Tibet through its affluents, and in fact drains the Tibetan provinces of Katshi, Kham, and Minyak. Szechuan became an empire in the third century after Christ, and the first capital city built near the Yangtze river was Chĕngtu. But after forty years it was again absorbed by the empire of North China. The river in arriving at Süchow at its most southern point receives the River of Golden Sand and the Yünnan traffic, and the union of the trade of two provinces greatly increases the number of sailing boats on the river. It turns to the north-east to proceed to Chungking, where the Pao river enters it, bringing with it the produce of northern Szechuan and rendering this prefectural city the greatest centre of trade in the province. The gorges occupy a hundred miles in extent. They have made the Yangtze celebrated as a poetic river, for the poets of China have been much stirred by them ; and those who disbelieve in the existence of imagination amongst the Chinese should visit the gorges before they decide whether it is possible for a literary nation to avoid becoming endowed with poetic creativeness, when nature herself compels them to this by her grandeur and solemnity. Issuing from its narrow channel the river flows now a mighty stream through five hundred miles of the province of Hupeh to Hankow, a country all under the control of the Wuchang viceroy. Its course is south-east while it bathes the walls of cities which were once the successive capitals of ancient kingdoms. The rainfall of Hunan province reaches the Tungting lake and contributes to feed the river. No scholarly native passes the mouth of the lake without thinking of the great poet who two

thousand years ago committed suicide here because he had fallen on evil times and was not allowed by his sovereign and cousin to conduct the government of the country in times of peculiar danger. After this the river trends to the north-east till it reaches Wuchang and Hankow, where the Han river enters it. It is at this point that the floods are highest and are an annual danger. The rise of water at Hankow is often fifty feet. The greatest danger is when rain has extended at one time over Hupeh represented by the Han river, Hunan, represented by the Tungting lake, and Szechuan and Tibet, represented by the Yangtze. The natural relief for floods is found in the Tungting lake, which affords a broad surface, and in the scouring power of the river which adds depth. At Hankow more lake surface is needed. It is an annual duty of the Viceroy to inspect the banks both of the Yangtze and of the Han. Hankow is the centre of China, and the river here presents to the eye a scene of wonderful activity. Higher up in Szechuan, it is said to bear on its waters five thousand boats in a year of a size varying from four and five to ninety tons each. The quantity of traffic at Hankow is many times greater. The merchants of eight provinces bring their wares here either by the Han or the Yangtze. Five hundred steamer visits are made here in a year and a thousand visits of sailing vessels, and they represent a trade whose value is between nine and ten million pounds sterling.

The course of the Yangtze in its remaining six hundred miles is first to the south-east to Kiukiang, where it has left Hupeh and has entered Kiangsi province, the rainfall of which it receives through the Poyang lake. It is a happy thing for the people that the lake here to a large extent prevents such flooding in seasons of heavy rain as takes place at Hankow. Every July the river is at the highest, and at that time the flood at Hankow is several feet higher than at any other part of the river. This seems to show the need at that port of artificial reservoirs into which a portion of the flood waters could be drawn off. At Kiukiang the scenery and historical recollections of the Lushan impart a special charm to this portion of the river. Kiukiang is the hottest among all the cities where Europeans reside in China. We next pass Wuhu, the centre of an immense rice trade, in the province of Anhui. The river at Anching and Wuhu has become bent to the north-east and the atmosphere is slightly cooler. Entering the province of Kiangsu the river reaches Nanking, the capital of several dynasties. Sun Chi-nan was the first who selected it, and he removed to this spot from Wuchang. It remained the capital of South China for about four centuries, with the occasional intermission of a few years. After its long wanderings the river reaches Chinkiang where the Grand Canal, constructed to convey the grain of the south to the capital, meets it. Here, too, the full force of the tide is felt, and the river soon becomes many miles wide. This enlarged breadth and the tide together render the mighty stream so much the more efficient in forming new land. It has more sea room and it spreads its burden of mud and sand more widely and evenly. Islands form quickly in the *embouchure.* Tsungming was not known before the Ming dynasty, and new islands are now in course of rapid formation. The tide carries every day a new supply of deposit up every creek, which contributes to raise the land on which the farmer labours. To this is added all the decaying vegetable matter which gives to the soil beneath the whole of those constituent parts which it does not breathe back ,into the atmosphere. Its work of land making done, the river returns at last to the sea, from which it originally came.

FÊNG-SHUI.

THE term Fêng-shui is applied to what is called the Wind and Water superstition of the Chinese. In selecting sites for graves and houses the professors of this false science describe the locality in their fashion and are allowed to give what advice they please and are paid as we pay a surveying engineer. The system came into China with Buddhism and still exists in India in a modified form. It is there prevalent among the native doctors, who teach that diseases are caused by wind and water. The Chinese have adopted the name, while they have changed its nature and made it specially referable to the selection of sites for ancestral worship and for graves. It is a modern fancy of the Chinese and is frequently discussed in native periodicals. It was elaborated early in the fourth century by Kwo-p'u, a learned man of Nanking, to which city he came from Shansi. He published a treatise in 20 sections called the Book of Burial. The modern Fêng-shui is here found in its elements, and eight of the twelve sections are still used by the professors of Fêng-shui as the basis of their theory. He was much influenced by the idea of lucky portents, which the new Buddhism had done everything to encourage. In his time the Chin Emperors came to live at Nanking, and Kwo-p'u was able to find a reason in its natural situation for the good fortune of the city. He believed he could foretell the destiny of any one by portents. He was beheaded before he was fifty, because he professed to be able to read the decrees of heaven on the destiny of individuals and refused to withhold his opinions. The high authorities of his day asked him, " To what age will you live? " " Till twelve o'clock this day," he answered, " when the life allotted to me will end." The angry personage he had offended issued the order that it should be as he had said. When led out to execution he made predictions saying that a certain tree would be found at the place of execution. At that tree a nest of a certain bird would be found. These statements are said to have been verified. He was a most learned man, a fine scholar, poet and critic. But such was the effect on him of the half

Babylonian, half Hindoo view of destiny, portents, and the influence of the stars then current, that he thought he could tell exactly what would happen to the descendants of anyone who was buried in a particular spot; and it was through his strong faith in his theory and in himself that he became the founder of Fêng-shui. After Kwo-pu's time the Fêng-shui of Fukien gradually became celebrated. It was very much directed to the construction and the selection of the locality of the ancestral temple. This system has had a considerable influence through its popularity with certain classes in Fukien and the neighbouring province of Chêkiang. The light and dark aspects observable in localities must not be mutually opposed. The influence of the five planets and of the Pakwa diagrams must be in harmony in order to secure life and victory. This system has of late lost ground. It is less influential than the Kiangsi system initiated by Yang Chiün-sung and three other Fêng-shui authors. Their talk is to a large extent of what they call the Dragon Hollow, the sand water and such things. This trifling with words without meaning is in vogue at present, although it is rated at its true value by every intelligent Chinese, whose disbelief unfortunately does not prevent its being extensively practised. Indeed, it is universally regarded as essential when a house is to be built or a grave to be opened. It is particularly prevalent in South China, and dates from the Sung dynasty. Unfortunately Chu Hi and Tsai Yuen-ting, a Prime Minister of the 12th century, gave the influence of their great names to support its credit among the people. The worship of ancestors was modified to suit the ideas of the Sung dynasty literati, of whom the two mentioned were among the most influential. The Government, even till a few years ago, supported the Fêng-shui theory although each individual member of the Government disbelieves it. In 1871 the Government prepared eight regulations for the management of matters connected with Christian Missions

in China. These regulations were not accepted by the foreign Ministers in Peking and consequently were laid aside like a lost bill in Parliament. In the eighth regulation it was proposed in all seriousness to refuse any site for a church if the magistrate thought the erection would be detrimental to the Fêng-shui, or good luck, of the neighbourhood. Thus it is shown that this superstition may creep into state papers and influence important government policy unless a watch is kept against it. Yet belief in it is denied by any one of position.

The present opponents of Fêng-shui say of it that it is an attempt to rob the spiritual beings in the universe of their knowledge, and to turn back the heavenly decree. By this they mean that the good and ill fortune of mankind are really controlled by Divine Providence, or by Heaven as they prefer to say, and that the selectors of sites for graves aim wrongfully to control the decrees of heavenly destiny. They aim to make a man's prosperity greater than it ought to be and his adversity less. But this is not their only objection to it. They say it causes great social inconvenience and injustice. If there is exceptional sickness in any locality just after a rich man has built a tomb or a house, the neighbours say it is his fault, and he must restore the good luck of the neighbourhood, or pay heavy damages as a compensation. The neighbours have the advantage of numbers in the trouble that ensues, which takes the form of a law suit or of a boycotting. This last consists of an intolerable warfare of words. The mulct on a rich family at the present time when unfortunately drawn into this position amounts to several hundred taels. In such neighbourhoods no one ventures to charge the professors of Fêng-shui with deception, nor the loud promoters of the popular delusion (who share among them the rich man's money) with pretending to believe in Fêng-shui for the sake of gain. But it is fortunate that the Chinese newspapers speak the truth on this point and that their ridicule of Fêng-shui does not injure their circulation. No intelligent Chinese really believes in it, and this secret unbelief is working out good results slowly. The influence of western science is making itself more and more felt every year, and missionary efforts are directed to the overthrow of this and kindred delusions, not without a good deal of useful effect. Every step taken by any Viceroy or Governor to found a foreign school or promote the circulation of scientific books and journals is driving a nail into the coffin of the Fêng-shui superstition. The sooner it is buried out of sight the better for China, for it is a mighty enemy to civilised progress and the true good of the people of this country.

◆

IRRIGATION.

FIFTY years ago, before the great destruction of opium by Lin Tse-hsü at Canton, this statesman had his mind very much bent towards the subject of irrigation. He was anxious to see the methods of rice cultivation now employed on the lower Yangtze extended to Chihli. In this he followed a policy which had from time to time been a favourite with preceding statesmen ever since the thirteenth century. In a memorial Lin states that this mode of cultivation had been very much in use in ancient times. In the first century of our era he mentions that close to Peking, under the mountains which bring down rivers from the plateau of Mongolia, there were 8,000 *ching* of land set apart for growing rice. If we estimate this area by the small measure of those times, which was about eight inches to the foot, it would amount to 60,000 acres or 100 square miles. Over this large extent of land a good official of those times persuaded the people to employ irrigation and grow rice. He told them this would make them rich. He did not add that this industry would also rapidly increase the population in that neighbourhood. The Chinese economists have always aimed at producing wealth, but they have persistently forgotten that it is

equally important to provide for the safety and well-being of the new mouths which increased grain production brings. In the third century a still larger area is spoken of in the same locality as the scene of active rice cultivation. Even a million *mow* of land are in one passage stated to have been under this cultivation. These citations occur in the valuable histories known as the *Hou Han-shu* and the *Wei-shu*, and in the famous work on Chinese rivers known as the *Shui Ching Chu* of the sixth century. These books are the principal historical authorities for that locality in that age. Coming down to the Sui dynasty the harvest of rice and millet is stated to have amounted in the same region to thousands of thousands of piculs, thus showing that the method of irrigation was then extensively practised there. At the same time a new effort was made to increase the productiveness of the region by adding 1,000 *ching*, which would probably be 10,000 acres. The Chinese estimate that an acre (six *mow*) will keep six persons in comfort if they sell part of the rice to buy clothing and tools and keep their houses in repair. If the 10,000 acres all belonged to poor people this would imply a population of 60,000 persons, but in fact much of the rice is turned into money, and added to the stores of the rich, while the rice sold is eaten at a distance. It may therefore be several years before the pressure from too great a population is felt. In the Yang dynasty we are told in history that 3,000 *ching* in a locality near Peking were under rice cultivation.

In the closing years of the tenth century the Sung dynasty made good its possession of the imperial authority. The Kietan Tartars at that time were in the habit of constantly invading Chihli, and the plan adopted to keep them in check was to make rice fields all the way for upwards of fifty miles east and west of Peking at the foot of the mountains. They were to be cultivated by soldiers, who were thus to support themselves by agricultural employment. An account of this system of frontier defence is given in the Sung

History. The tract of land was north and south about twenty miles wide, and east and west more than a hundred miles long. Banks were made to retain the water necessary for irrigation, and the soldiers who kept them in repair were always in readiness for the mounted Tartar horsemen when they came on robbing excursions down the passes on to the cultivated lands of China. Many objections were raised, but the promoter of the scheme quoted the old histories, and won the emperor's approval. He was himself appointed to be in charge of the undertaking. Beyond the rice lands on the west were troops placed to guard the passes on the old system.

The real rice land of China is on the banks of the Yangtze in Anhui and Kiangsu. Irrigation is here easy and labour cheap. The cheapest rice to be found is that of Anhui. Over large portions of the rice producing country women share in the work of cultivation in planting out the young rice plants and in working the chain of buckets which pumps water into the fields. The competency of the women in this industry materially helps to lower the price of labour. As a reward they are not obliged to bind their feet. The annual product is very large and Wuhu is now able to help both the northern and southern provinces when in need. When lately the summer floods of Chihli became so overwhelming as to render many thousands homeless and destitute, leading to a decree that southern merchants should be invited to ship rice to Tientsin free of duty, the Canton and Fukien merchants resident in Wuhu telegraphed at once (so the native newspapers say) for steamers to Shanghai and the south, so that they might be able to respond to this demand. The Yangtze river is thus seen to be of immense value by the aid it gives, in the irrigation of the rice fields, in saving the lives of the people in distant provinces. The usual time of floods is July, and during this month and August the rice fields act as lakes to draw off part of the overflow. Thus rice cultivation helps also as a direct agent in lowering the level of the summer flood waters in the rivers and in protecting the embankments from being broken through.

THE FLOODS IN THE NORTH.

THE summer rains in North-China have been specially abundant* and have brought on calamitous floods at very many points. The homes of the people over an immense region have been destroyed. The breaches in the Peiho, the Yellow River, the Grand Canal, and other rivers in Chihli and Shantung are so numerous that the officers in charge must be in despair. The whole country is a vast alluvial flat intersected by rivers and spotted by lake hollows of all dimensions. If the observer take his stand at Tientsin and look north-west towards the capital there are several breaches in the Peiho all the way to Pukou, fifteen miles distant. The water of the flooded plain on the right bank may be seen at one point falling as a cascade into the river with a drop of two feet. Then crossing the river it rushes into the fields beyond through the left bank. All around crops are overwhelmed, houses overthrown, and the population scattered. The rivers meeting at Tientsin from the north-west and south have caused this. Human labour has elevated the city out of the reach of floods, and the embankments and raised roads afford a refuge to fugitives. Otherwise all that is seen is one vast sea. It was so a generation ago in a former year of heavy rain and it will be so after a generation again. But it is not an evil which science cannot mitigate, and great is the responsibility of the high officers who, having the administrative control of the inundated regions, refuse to change old traditions and to invite help from those who know. On the south of the city for thirty miles no dry land is seen. In other directions the same is true for a hundred miles. In many parts the water on the plain finds no outlet and will remain to be slowly evaporated. Only after about three years, it is supposed, will all this

----

* Written in September, 1890.

country be dry land again. If we remove our point of observation beyond Paoting-fu, 150 miles west of Tientsin, there is a large inundated tract towards Hwailu where the mountains are crossed into Shansi. Proceeding to the south-west the Grand Canal coming from the south is identical with the old Wei river for about 150 miles, entering that river at Linching. The Wei, above its confluence with the Grand Canal, flows from the mountains at the south end of Shansi for another 150 miles, and it is the rainfall of northern Honan and of the mountains of southern Shansi that has just now swelled this river and the Grand Canal. There is a closed lock at the confluence at Linching which is opened occasionally to allow the grain junks to pass on their way to Tientsin from the south. This year the water of the Wei was high enough at one time to flow over the lock into the Shantung or southern portion of the Canal. Not far below this point at Wucheng the bank has been forced in several places and the country inundated. In consequence the crops are ruined and the people must starve. In all there are said to be twenty-two breaks in the embankment of the Canal between Linching and Tientsin. There has been, it is said, no such inundation in this part of Shantung since 1822. The Wei River has risen eight feet and this is the chief cause of the flood which has now swept away whole villages by a sudden rush, not allowing a large part of the inhabitants time to escape. An immense number are believed to have been drowned.

The cry of distress is now heard not only from Tientsin and the ports bordering on the canal. The Yellow River in Shantung nearer the sea on the 7th and 8th of July burst its banks a little to the north-west of Chinan, the provincial capital, in a violent storm of wind and rain. It is stated that the strength of the blast raised the waters so high that they overcame all obstacles and caused the removal of 300 feet of embankment on the north side of the river. The sea is distant about 120 miles from this point. An immense body of water was thus thrown on the plain belonging to Wutingfu, the most northern prefecture of Shantung near the sea. Many districts which during the last few years have not been reached by the floods are now covered with water in this part, and the crops on them hopelessly destroyed. In this case the evil was want of strength in the embankment, which needs to be made proof against the July freshet joined with heavy rain such as characterised this year, armed with the force of a violent storm. At the end of last year the river showed its power by forcing a new way for itself by a fresh route to the sea near its mouth. At that time it made a détour to the north, deserting the channel assigned it by the officials in charge, at a point about 20 miles from the sea. This new channel was accepted by the officials, and their action was approved by the emperor. At the new outbreak, a hundred miles further up the stream, it will be more difficult to bring the river under control, because it has become, with its one outlet to the ocean recently made, more winding than before. The Mississippi engineering is based on the principle that the outlet should be straight and short. The Chinese have allowed the unconscious stream to choose its own path just as the height of the freshet, the local level, and the winds and storms of the hour compelled it. All ought to be set right by the engineers of the West applying the most approved principles in modern engineering. It certainly seems reasonable that, considering the vast extent of level country in that part of China, as many as possible straight outlets to the sea should be provided, each of them well banked. Then when the July freshet, the peach blossom freshet in April, and the autumn freshet in August, come in force, the rising swell of water will be carried quickly past before it can do harm, to the sea, its natural home. Whatever can be done to lower the swell in the time of freshets must be done. Up the stream there must be irrigation reservoirs; near the mouth there should be straight channels to the sea. Labour is cheap and abundant in China, but it needs skilled superintendence. China must consent to use foreign experts. Such men as the English engineers who banked the mouths of the Danube, the Americans who did the same for the Mississippi, or the Dutch who keep the Rhine under control, would be likely if employed to save an immense future outlay to the government by bringing under a safe system the rivers of Chihli and Shantung.

THE CHINESE TREATMENT OF CHOLERA.

MANY Chinese doctors well remember the cholera of 1860 and 1862. They keep account of both these years as times when this fell disease was most destructive of human life in their country. A leading article in one of the Shanghai daily newspapers in Chinese, written by a well-informed native physician, gives the views of his class on the treatment that should be regarded as most suitable. He starts with saying that most men who die from cholera owe their death not so much to the disease itself as to the incompetency of the native doctors in attendance. They do not attend to the real nature of the disease, and they treat only its outer manifestation. Then, he says, in persons attacked there is a lack of healthy strength and a liability to fatigue. They get hot by day by exposure, and sleep in draughts by night unprotected. Such persons if they take food at irregular intervals and sometimes go with empty stomachs, are predisposed for cholera, which may enter with the breath through the lungs and the stomach, thus passing into the intestines. The way he puts it is peculiar. The lungs control the skin and hair. The violent perspiration shows that the lungs are affected, as the vomiting shows that the stomach is disordered. The spasms indicate that the liver is affected, because the muscles are under the control of that organ. If a good doctor is not called soon the liver will be reached and spasms will begin. Should wise

treatment still be delayed the heart and spleen will be affected and then the tongue will curl up and death will ensue. Sometimes the process is quicker and death occurs after from two to four hours. This is because the evil influence entering from without strikes directly into the seat of the "cold principle" in the lower intestines.

This physician then proceeds to describe his own, as he says, very successful mode of treating cholera. He notices seven symptoms—vomiting, diarrhœa, low pulse, cold limbs, perspiration, spasms, and exhaustion. He at once orders from the druggist a prepared dose to be heated at the patient's house and taken warm to the extent of a good sized tea-cupful. In this dose the main things are such drugs as ginger, ginseng, Chinese cardamoms and a sort of carraway seed. After this the patient receives *atractylodes alba*, called *peshu* by the apothecaries, a medicine of which the Chinese think a great deal as an aromatic tonic and stimulant. They use it in cases of profuse sweating and apoplexy, chronic dysentery, and rheumatism. It belongs to the *cynaraceœ* among the species of which are found many plants known in Europe as furnishing useful stomachic and febrifuge medicines. If the disease progresses still into the spasmodic state with numbness of the limbs this physician would use *pœonia albiflora*, the *pecho* of the native apothecaries, with *boymia rutœcarpa*, and a pepperwort which they call *wuchuyü*. Our druggists know it by the name *xanthoxylum piperitum*. It is one of the commoner aromatic stimulants in China and in Japan. To this he adds cinnamon bark.

In 1861-1863, he remarks, when the cholera reached Shanghai, it was a time when the people were crowded indiscriminately in an insufficient number of dwellings. Refugees had arrived in thousands, escaped from the daily scenes of burning and fighting which were witnessed over all the adjoining country at that time. He notices that the sanitary conditions were such that the people were specially liable to be attacked by cholera. It was then that this physician tried his methods and experience. As he does not mention any preparation of opium or of mercury he is probably a cautious doctor and would avoid strong remedies. We should expect opium to be applied to soothe the extraordinary derangement of the system when under the dominion of cholera. Instead of this he gives pig's liver mixed with brick dust from the inside of a furnace, a mixture honoured with the title *Fulung-kan*, " liver of the hiding dragon."* To this are added one or two ounces of ginger. This remedy of his has had great popularity with many persons and been very successful. He has had, he tells us, a large practice during the summer of this year and the effect on patients of his remedies has been such as to give him great satisfaction. He could not secure this popularity without favouring the popular beliefs.

He then tells what other doctors say about the treatment and origin of cholera. Its not being mentioned, that is, under the name *sha*, in early books has excited much remark. It first occurs in a book which recommends in treating it the use of paper from which silkworms have retired, *ts'an t'ui chih.* This book is probably of the Ming dynasty, for he proceeds to say that the cholera came in the middle of the 17th century with the dynasty from Manchuria spreading from the north southward. He notices the use of the name "Manchurian sickness" and of " the foreign cholera." If this is so it is a curious fact in the history of the disease, and the " Manchurian sickness" needs to be inquired into. It seems more likely that Europe is right in supposing that cholera originated in the hot jungles of southern Asia, and at a more recent date than this account states. The same word *sha* is applied to diphtheria and scarlet fever, which became epidemic in China in the severest form in 1733, and belong to the winter and spring. The word *sha* is applied to some five or six

diseases, in part summer and autumn epidemics, like cholera, and in part prevailing in the winter and spring. All have appeared in China in the 17th, 18th, or 19th centuries for the first time. The term *ho loan*, also applied to different kinds of cholera, is an ancient name, descriptive of it in the old times when it was not yet epidemic. The reader will judge for himself as to the drugs the names of which have been mentioned above. They are really not very different from what are found in western practice. Chinese doctors appear from what is here said to be fond of using mild remedies, while they avoid those which are very powerful in their operation; as to the nature of the medicines, they are on the whole much the same as our own.

THE CLIMATE OF CHINA.

THE clouds which bring rain to China come from the sea and receive their burden of moisture by evaporation over the Pacific Ocean. Winds from the north and west are usually rainless because of the small amount of watery surface on which the heat of the sun can operate. The climate of China has high maxima and low minima of heat and cold. In Peking the greatest cold is four and a half degrees above zero, according to Fritsche, our best authority on climate, and the greatest heat ninety-seven. At Shanghai the greatest cold is about seventeen degrees and the greatest heat a hundred and two. At Canton the cold increases till it is a degree above freezing point in winter and there ceases. The greatest heat in that latitude is ninety-three. At Foochow in the winter the thermometer indicates two degrees above freezing point when at its lowest. At the same place the maximum heat in summer is ninety-seven. The greatest difference between summer heat and winter cold is at Peking, where it amounts to nearly ninety-three degrees. The inhabitants of Shanghai experience a difference of eighty-five degrees during the year. At Foochow the difference is sixty-three degrees and at Canton sixty. The people need to be better

---

* Hot remedies must be used. The fire god of whom the "hiding dragon" is one of the titles, is supposed to have put his influence into the furnace brickwork.

armed against winter cold in the north than elsewhere. The great comfort of the poor in the north is a sheep skin to wrap round them in winter. It is procured from Mongolia, and if they have not this they have wadded cotton. It is distance from the sea which causes the difference between summer and winter to be so great as it is in North China. So also it is proximity to the sea joined with the mountainous character of the adjacent country which tends to equalise the climate at Canton and Foochow. The sea warms the air in winter and the mountains cool it in summer. In the north on the contrary the level plains are very little cooled by the few mountains which exist, and there is no sea to warm the air in winter.

One of the chief official duties of the Chinese Emperor is to pray for rain and snow in certain temples. The absence of moisture over the wide extent of Mongolia limits the supply of moisture, because, for instance, in the winter the prevailing wind is from the north and that wind is dry. Snow is needed for the wheat crop which is sown in the autumn, and rain in spring and summer for the various kinds of millet. A year seldom passes in which the Emperor does not proceed more than once to the temples to pray either for snow or for rain. The uncertainty of the rainfall is one of the great misfortunes of North China, and it is attended by another almost equally destructive, the danger from floods. Whenever there is heavy rain in North China there may be also a superabundant rainfall in Mongolia and Tibet. This the northern provinces of China receive through their rivers. The rivers by carrying along with them stones, sand, and silt are always raising the plains higher. On this account they cannot keep the same course but must occupy in succession all parts of the plains which they traverse and to the height of which they are constantly adding a little. The summer monsoon causes the winds to blow from the south-east, and this is so in the north and in the south of China. The rain clouds of China are brought by the south-east winds, changing occasionally to south and south-

west; and from the same south-east quarter come the typhoons which are an annual terror to Chinese navigation.

From the same part of the ocean, near the Philippine Islands on the north-east, which originates the typhoons, and in part the monsoon, flows the warm water current which bathes the shores of Japan, and is called by the Japanese the Kurosiwo. This is a part of the northern equatorial current of geographers which comes across the Pacific ocean from America in a westerly direction, and is diverted northward by the Philippine Islands. But for the Philippine Islands and Formosa, which cause this current to take a sharp angle to the north, China would have a warmer climate. As it is the Kurosiwo makes the Philippines and Formosa more tropical, and then moves in the direction of Japan and Corea. Its effect on Japan is to render the climate mild enough for the silk and tea industries to flourish there. The same isothermal line which passes through the silk and tea districts south of the Yangtze river in China crosses the ocean to Nagasaki, which is about five degrees north of these districts, and then proceeds, still with an incline to the north, towards Osaka and Tokio. The south coast of Japan has thus the same temperature as Foochow and Hangchow, because Japan is in the midst of the sea and is bathed on both sides by the Kurosiwo current. Corea also on its western coast is warmed somewhat by the same current, which sends a branch in that direction. The sea coast of Chinese Tartary is bathed by a cold water current flowing from Kamschatka in the far north and continuing to Corea, which it cools on the east coast. Corresponding to this cold current is another which flows out of the Gulf of Pechili and proceeds alongside of the China coast as far as to the Formosa Channel. The temperature of this current is given by Fritsche as fifty-nine in February and seventy-nine in September a little to the north of Formosa. A few degrees further to the east the water of the ocean is seventy degrees in February and in July eighty-eight.

Between Corea and Japan the temperature of the water of the sea is eighty-two degrees Fahrenheit in August and sixty-one in June. This mildness of the temperature is caused by the warm water current, in the benefit of which China does not share. Japan has moisture and verdant beauty. China has continental regularity of temperature and freedom from abrupt changes. The annual progress from heat to cold and from cold to heat, gradual as it is, probably favours the physical development of the Chinese and helps to render them industrious, steady and not given to change.

CHINESE EDUCATIONAL COLLEGES.

THE new collegiate institutions founded by the Customs Taotais of Shanghai are an index to the present state of education among the Chinese. The gift of 20,000 taels by Yin Taotai, twenty - four years ago, gave origin to the *Lung-men-shu-yuen*. It has 36 pupils or beneficiaries and they include Masters of Arts, Bachelors of Arts and some of the rank of *Kung sheng*, intervening between these degrees. The subject of study is philosophy. This is not, however, the philosophy of mind as we understand it, nor is it anything so charming as Plato or Cicero would have called philosophy. It is the philosophy of the Sung dynasty known as the *Sing-li*, founded by the great writers of that time, the 11th and 12th centuries. It is a moral philosophy combining into a system the teaching of the Chinese sages on ethical subjects, on the origin of heaven and earth, and on man's place in nature. These philosophers had read Buddhist and Taoist books, and the traces of this reading and of their historical and literary culture are seen in the system of philosophy elaborated by them and still in vogue. The Emperor Hien-feng favoured it and probably this is the reason that Yin Taotai thought it would be a good thing for the interests of learning at Shanghai to promote its study among the graduates. There is an annual in-

come of 480 ounces of silver to maintain the students at the College, where they have rooms for residence.

There is also an examining college called the *Chiu-chih-shu-yuen*, founded sixteen years ago at the beginning of the reign of Kuang-hsü by Fêng Taotai. A sum of 600 ounces of silver from the interest of the capital is devoted to the payment of four examiners. They issue questions and subjects for essays every quarter, examine the papers sent in by competitors and assign prizes. The first examiner propounds questions in classical study and poetry and literature generally. The second examines in history and subjects connected with the administration of public affairs both local and national, the third examines is mathematics and the fourth in geography. No recognition of the importance of the English language is found in the programme of subjects. Only the Chinese language is used, the object being to promote high studies with the use of Chinese text books. Two months and a half are allowed for answering the questions or discussing the subjects proposed. The best writer receives a prize of five taels, the second best has four taels. The writer standing third receives $3\frac{1}{2}$ taels, the fourth has three taels, the fifth two and the sixth one. Smaller sums are given to the inferior essayists. The scope of the questions embraces modern learning. While the *Lung-men* college favours Sung dynasty studies, this college favours the study of books by more modern authors and the subjects included are rather critical and historical than philosophical. Fêng Taotai thought that the philosophy of the Sung dynasty was less important than to have the graduates versed in history and in all practical matters connected with local and general government. This system promotes the reading of modern books. Able men arm themselves with the necessary knowledge from various new publications read expressly. They cannot discuss the subjects propounded in so satisfactory a way as to gain a prize unless they read contemporary documents and authors. The stimulus of prizes has in the west long been used in schools to excite the activity of the mental faculties of boys and girls. Now the same system is being applied to promote self-education in after life. The system is only beginning in the west and in China. It is a movement full of promise. Self-education by reading in the unoccupied hours of the day is assisted by every offer of prizes open to general competition, because the stimulus leads to mental work in connection with the subject of the books read. The professors in our universities at home are now becoming guides in study to groups of readers beyond the circle of their college classes. This is effected by the establishment of reading circles. Every one has heard of the Chautauqua system in America where the self-education of readers of mature age, members of reading circles, is aided by summer camp meetings for lectures and examinations. This is what the Anglo-Saxon race is doing at home. It is a matter of great interest to see in China an effort like this of voluntary examinations with prizes by which readers are stimulated to study a great variety of modern books, and actually to take part themselves in the thinking of the age by composing essays on subjects which familiarise them with the modern currents of opinion. Stimulus is needed. Readers take refuge in novels from the want of interest attaching to more useful books. If they write an essay or a poem on a given subject and an examiner or a committee are to read that essay and award a prize to it if it is deserved, then books of solid information will be preferred to some unhealthy romance. Fiction tires the mental faculties by straining them too much. It is too exciting. This is true for the Anglo-Saxon and for the Chinese. Sober useful reading is better ; and in order to encourage the habit of reading useful books, the composition of essays in their subjects should also be encouraged.

The Taotai who spent thirty thousand taels (£7,000) on the formation of an examining college probably did better than his predecessor who spent £5,000 on the foundation of a college providing free board and lodging for thirty-six select students. Yet the benefit arising from this last institution is not small : men from all the neighbouring cities are chosen after examination and reside together in free quarters with the advantage of a large and well chosen library. They can improve their knowledge and compete for prizes in the other college or for the Viceroy's prizes if they wish; by reading modern works their horizon is widened, and they learn to think and write with more culture and force. The country thus obtains an increase in its staff of able writers. Almost all the able men now in the higher posts in various parts of China appear to be aware of the great need for promoting the higher education. Li Hung-chang and Chang Chih-tung are pushing their influence in this direction. Among the Taotai posts in connection with foreign trade, Ningpo has an examining college the programme of which is very much like that at Shanghai. At the latter place there are usually about a hundred competitors. In mathematics there are only five or six. Twenty or thirty or it may be forty write for the prizes in classical criticism and poetry. As many more write upon history and on administrative questions. In geography, including cities, rivers, and local products, as well as map-making, there are not so many.

THE MARINER'S COMPASS A CHINESE INVENTION.

THERE have been some new indications in Europe of a desire to know the facts regarding the claim of the Chinese to have invented the' mariner's compass. A professor in Vienna is now making inquiries on this matter. Dr. Chalmers, of Hongkong, has gone over the older passages in the literature and in the *China Review* and shown that in ancient times the Chinese had not yet begun to use the mariner's compass. Mr. Mayers drew attention to the same subject and noticed that there is no reference to it in the early voyages of which we have any account. The Chinese used the needle in land carriages but did not think of applying it to navigation. As to one thing there can be no doubt; the Chinese did not learn the properties of a magnetised needle from any other country. They found it out for themselves, though it is impossible to point to the man by name who first observed that a magnetised needle points north and south. Doubtless it came about in this way. The Chinese as we know have in their country boundless tracts of ironstone, and among these no small portion is magnetic. Every woman needs a needle, and iron early took the place of the old stone needles and were commonly used before the time of Ch'in Shih-huang, that is, more than 21 centuries ago. Whenever a needle happened to be made of magnetic iron it might reveal its south-pointing quality by falling into a cup of water, when it happened to be attached to a splinter of wood, for example. It came in some such way to be known commonly that certain needles had this quality. The great producing centre for magnetic iron is T'szchou, in southern Chihli. This city was very early called the City of Mercy, and the magnetic stone produced there came to be known as the stone of T'szchou, and so *t'sz shih* became the ordinary name for a magnet. Later the Chinese began to speak of the city as the "City of the Magnet" instead of calling it the "City of Mercy." The polarity of the magnetic needle would become known to the Chinese of that city and its neighbourhood first. The first who noticed the polarity would be some intelligent person who communicated the fact as an inaccountable peculiarity in an age when omens and portents were diligently sought for in every natural object and phenomenon. Kwei Ku-tsz, the earliest author who mentions the south-pointing needle, lived in the 4th century before Christ. There can be no reasonable doubt that the polarity of the needle was known at that time. Whatever myth regarding the needle was invented would be based on the knowledge of the physical fact, and the discovery of the fact must have preceded the invention of any myth embracing it. As to the discovery, there is no reason to suppose it was in any way foreign, because the Chinese use an enormous number of needles and have an inexhaustible supply of ironstone. There is no need to say a word in favour of India because that country has no iron to speak of. But though the polarity was known, we do not find that it was turned to a practical use till the Tsin dynasty, when landscapes began to be studied by the professors of *fêngshui*. There was at that time a general belief in the magical powers of natural objects. This was a Buddhist doctrine and it took firm hold on the Chinese mind of that age. Just as Buddhists believe that indications of the influence of Buddha are present everywhere in the natural world, so the Chinese philosophers of those times taught that indications of good and ill luck are to be seen all through nature. The polarity of the needle would take its place in this category of thought. Though it is not distinctly mentioned by Ko Hung or by Kwo Pu in the fourth century, yet to the disciples of Kwo Pu it became an essential part of the landscape compass which the professors of *fêngshui* all use. Kwo Pu, the founder of this system, died A.D. 324, and it was not till four centuries later that the *fêngshui* compass began to assume its present form. Though Kwo Pu's fame is great as a believer in the doctrine that portents of future kings are to be found in the localities where they will subsequently be born, he left much to be done by others, and the compass used by the *fêngshui* professors for marking landscape indications was really first made about the eighth century by Chiu Yen-han. The compass was of hard wood, about a foot wide, and it had in the centre a small well in which a magnetised needle floated on water. On the compass were inscribed several concentric circles as on the wooden horizon of our globes. They embrace the twelve double hours, the ten denary symbols, the eight diagrams of Fuhi and other marks. This compass was used in preparing a *fêngshui* report of any spot where a house or tomb was to be constructed, so that the construction might not be upon an unlucky site or planned in an unlucky manner. At the same time there was living a Chinese who had studied Hindoo astronomy. This was Yi-hing, who was the imperial astronomer and also a Buddhist priest. He noticed that the needle did not point exactly north and that there was a variation of 2° 95'. This variation went on increasing till a century later, that is, till the ninth century. A professor of *fêngshui* named Yang-yi then added a new circle to the compass. On this improved compass the first of the twelve hours begins on the new circle at 7½° east of north. The compass it will be observed grew out of the old astrological report or nativity paper calculated from the position of stars, and prepared in the Han dynasty by astrologers as a regular part of social life, especially when marriages were about to be solemnised. Some of the old astronomical circles are preserved in the new *fêngshui* chart. This was the compass used when Shen-kwa wrote on the south-pointing needle in the 11th century. This author mentions that any iron needle acquires polarity by rubbing it on a piece of load-stone. He alludes to the variation as a fact which he himself had observed and speaks of the south-pointing needle as an implement used by the professors of *fêngshui*. By them it was employed in the form of a float upon water. After this, in A.D. 1122, Sü-king, the ambassador to Corea, describes the use of the floating needle on board ship while he made the voyage. This is the first instance, the earliest by more than a century, of the use of the mariner's compass on board ship found as yet in any book native or foreign. The book is called *Shih-kao-li-lu*, "Narrative of a Mission to Corea." The existence of this book settles the question of the first use of the mariner's compass at sea, in favour of the Chinese. At that time the needle floated on water supported by a piece of wood,

but in the Ming dynasty some Japanese junks engaged in piracy were captured by the Chinese, and the compass in use on board was found to have the needle dry and raised on-a-pivot, while still pointing southward. The Japanese had learned from Portuguese navigators to make a compass of this kind, and probably the needles they used were brought from Europe. From this time the Chinese adopted the principle of a pivot, and made their compasses without a well of water in the middle to float the needle in. Charts were probably used of a very rough kind, but. how far is not known. What we know is that the junkmaster was aware of the direction on his compass towards which he must steer to reach the port to which he was going. In the Sung dynasty, embracing part of the 10th as well as the 11th, 12th and part of 13th centuries, Chinese junks went to Persia and India. The Arabs trading to China directly would learn at that time the use of the compass and would apply it on board their dhows. From them the Europeans learned this useful invention. The credit of the discovery both of the polarity of a magnetised needle and its suitability for use by mariners at sea must be given to China. It was China also that has the credit of having first noticed that any iron needle may be polarised by rubbing it with a magnet. In the 13th century the Arabs used a floating compass on their dhows. The needle was made to float on the water by attaching it crosswise to a cornstalk or splinter of wood. A magnet applied to it drew it into a north and south direction. They would use western notation to mark the quarters and intermediate points on the horizon. When therefore the mariner's compass was adopted from them, the Chinese 24 points were not communicated. In the European compass the notation of 32 points is western, and rests on the winds and the sun. In the Chinese primitive mariner's compass the notation is that of the professors of *fêng-*

shui and rests on the old astrological division of the horizon into twelve double hours. From the Arab account we learn, what the Chinese accounts do not tell us, that the Chinese floated the needle by inserting it in a splinter of wood.

———◆———

THE USE OF COTTON YARN.

ONE main cause of the rapid growth of Chinese population is found in the manufacturing industries of the country. Large towns are formed by the addition of manual labour of various kinds carried on in buildings other than those devoted to the sale of produce. The basis of the social fabric is in agriculture. Where great rivers by silt form wide reaches of fertile land more grain is grown than the growers can themselves use. A market town springs up where the superfluity of food is sold for articles which merchants bring. A shopkeeping class is then required. Some of the sons of agriculturists meet this need by establishing themselves at the market. Clothing and other articles are brought for a time from a distance. But at last some one who has capital introduces spinning wheels and looms. The agricultural population furnishes another contingent of spinners and weavers; dyers and threadmakers follow; bricklayers and carpenters, butchers and bakers, the fowler and the fisherman multiply. Ironmongery is regularly supplied and renders blacksmiths a necessity. All the other trades follow by a law of inevitable increase to supply all the ever-growing wants of an expanding population. Thus the large cities of the great Soochow plain are accounted for. As occupations multiply marriages follow and new families are added to the community with great rapidity.

The Chinese began to wear cotton clothing from six to seven hundred years ago. They had looms before for silk, satin and grass cloth. They were able to adapt the silk loom to cotton weaving, and it was carried on as a new industry in parts of the country where the cotton plant grows. This new art found occupation for persons in regions not favouring the cultivation of the mulberry, of hemp, and of the *dolichos*, of which last the fabric known as grass cloth is made. This is the same that by the Chinese is called from its coolness "summer cloth." The spread of the cotton plant has been very rapid because it grows in the northern provinces where the winters are cold as well as in the south where the air is mild at the close of the year. The number of weavers increased with this new industry and of spinners also. Silk would be woven probably in less quantity and of better quality than before. It became the clothing of the rich, while cotton cloth became the clothing of the poor, because it could be more cheaply made. Just now this love of the people for new industries is gratified by the introduction of Indian yarn sent to China from the new spinning mills of Bombay. It comes at a time when through the great increase of population the people are becoming less able to buy dear clothing. The Indian yarn is suited to make coarse fabrics which are strong and wear well. It is now imported for weavers, for examples, in the eastern part of Canton province where there has not been much weaving before. It is also purchased for Kiangsi through Kiukiang, and much of the yarn imported through Swatow reaches the same province. It is not fine enough for the Shanghai weavers but it is prized at Chefoo and in Chihli. It will doubtless spread more widely because of the demand in certain provinces for cheap and coarse cloth. In future the demand for the finer native nankeens at a fair price will be met by home-grown cotton. But where the people through wages being too low are anxious to clothe their families with a strong coarse material, the new manufacture from Indian yarn will exactly suit the market, the more so because in China looms are a piece of cottage furniture and can be used when the weather prevents out-door occupations. Money can be earned at home by the industrious and this is felt to be an inestimable advantage by those who working for low wages are anxious never to be idle. Near Shanghai the cotton weavers are women in almost all cases. There is no pattern needing to be woven in. The person who throws the shuttle does all the work of the loom. Women begin to throw the shuttle and to practise the other manipulations at fourteen years of age. The cotton weaving industry is therefore in China eminently a female industry. This is not the case with silk and satin. In these men are the workers, two are always required, and the loom is very complex. The spread therefore of the use of Indian yarn in all parts of China is a testimony to the industry of the women.

The desire felt for a cheap cloth woven by the people at their own homes, if we embrace in our view the whole country, is greatest at Canton and its neighbourhood. For in Lappa in 1889 100,000 piculs of Indian yarn were imported, while 70,000 were imported at Canton. Pakhoi imported 93,000 piculs and Swatow 80,000. The value of the yarn bought by that province was five million taels. A large part of the import was forwarded to Yünnan and Kiangsi. In Yünnan many of the aborigines are purchasers and they weave with the material a cloth which they prefer for their own wear. In the far north Indian yarn is also becoming a great favourite. During the year 1889 Chihli, Shantung and Moukden bought three million taels' worth or 150,000 piculs. The desire felt for it in Central China is much weaker; all the ports on the Yangtze including Shanghai purchase only as much as Tientsin alone. New manufactures are thus seen to be spreading in the north and south while the centre is somewhat at a standstill. Altogether China purchased in 1889 about £3,000,000 worth of Indian yarn, thus shewing that she will weave if others will spin. The value last year of the cotton yarn imported

at Pakhoi, a small port, was more than half of all the imports taken together. The value of the yarn imported into Canton, a large port, stood next to that of opium among the imports. It was so at Swatow also. At some other southern ports cotton yarn stood after rice, opium and kerosene oil. China greatly values cheapness and if she can procure these she will supply her own coarse textile fabrics for the time by the cottage loom system and suit her own taste in strength and quality. The trade with China carried on by foreign countries is thus shown to be elastic. She can produce silk to supply European looms and she is prepared to buy cotton yarn from spinners at Bombay to meet the demand of her own population for coarse nankeens. For many years it seemed as if India could furnish only one article which China desired. Another article has now been found thus showing that in due time there will be little difficulty in substituting for opium, goods for which China will be grateful. It will be well too if China should learn that her best policy is to cultivate solidarity of interests with outside nations. Her aim should not be to become independent of foreign raw materials and foreign manufactures. It should rather be to buy what suits her from other nations and to sell to other nations what suits them. China's true interest will be found in the cultivation of universal brotherhood with the rest of mankind.

CHINESE AND FOREIGN MEDICINE.

THE appearance of a preface by the renowned Viceroy Li Hung-chang to a work on Therapeutics translated by Dr. Hunter of Chiningchow, may be taken as a sign of the times. The most influential man in China gives the prestige of his name to medical mission work in China and to the introduction into his country of foreign medical treatises. There is every reason to hope that the art of healing in China will now make some progress and take a higher standing. The medical literature of Chinese physicians will require to undergo some change to adapt itself to the new conditions. Native medicine will need to change its front somewhat, because China is beginning to review her time-honoured theories, and if necessary replace them by new ones. The prompt settlement of the Audience Question at about the same time when this preface was written is not without its lesson. The writer of the preface was a party to the policy which determined that the Emperor might without any difficulty receive the foreign envoys annually at the New Year. The writer of this preface is also conscious of defects in native medicine and wishes to see foreign methods of healing, and discoveries in the anatomy and physiology of the human frame, introduced into the practice of the native physicians.

Viceroy Li commences with an extract from Pan-koo. This author in his History of the early Han dynasty has a chapter on books, containing the oldest book catalogue possessed by China. The medical section of this catalogue like all the other sections gives the names of a considerable number of books since lost. Though the books are now no longer accessible, we can judge by their titles what they were. We learn from them that the Divine Husbandman, the Yellow Emperor, and the physician Yu-fu, were the first teachers of medicine in the opinion of China in A.D. 100. The names of thirty-nine treatises are given. There were books on fever, on diet, on modes of cure, on surgery, on massage, on the stone knife, on *Pien-tsio* and the pulse, on paralysis, and apoplexy, beside seven more general works on the healing art. Of these only two are now in existence. Pan-koo writing 1,800 years ago knew of these thirty-nine works. Their titles show the nature of medical practice in the hands of the ancient physicians. They cauterised, they felt the pulse, they

used the stone lancet. Strangely enough, they gave up the lancet after a few centuries, but kept to pulse-feeling and cauterisation still. They had fewer drugs then than now and they were simples taken in the form of warm decoctions. The bodily structure of man was described in the same way then as it is now. Two of Pan-koo's books are still read and they contain the old medical theory. What Pan-koo read, our Viceroy has read, and both read believingly. The Viceroy has quoted in the preface the exact words of both of these books as he has also quoted the exact words of Pan-koo in speaking of them. China of the present will not willingly let go the ideas of the China of the past. These two books, the *Soo-wen* and *Ling-choo*, are the Hippocrates and Galen of Chinese medicine. All well-informed Chinese readers are acquainted with them. The Viceroy has read them with admiration, but he is surrounded and pressed upon by the influences of the modern period. He has seen and helped in the work of the medical missionaries in Tientsin. He has read translated works on chemistry, physiology, physics, botany and various other subjects, and he has no idea of doubting foreign science. He accepts it, but he will not throw aside the old native books. In this preface he does not say whether he still believes in the Yin and Yang principles or not. But he probably does. It would be very difficult for any Chinese to think of fever and not regard it as an undue prevalence of fire, or of dropsy without picturing it to himself as an instance of the water element becoming too powerful. The physician is a man who by the use of judicious methods can restore equilibrium among the five elemental powers which exist together in the body of a sick man, and have become disturbed in their action. We do not wonder therefore if in this preface the writer says that he has read Jacob Rho's work on anatomy with particular pleasure. That book was written more than two centuries ago. The doctrine of the four elements still existed then in European science, and this would naturally render a book on anatomy in that age easier of acceptance to a Chinese reader, because the theory would be more like his own. The Viceroy mentions in closing that the book now translated is strictly on the art of healing. He advises readers not to reject it as strange, but to look on it as a work valuable enough to be treasured like a treatise of Ko-hung or Sun Sze-miao, and carefully studied for practical use. He concludes by saying that if the medical student will join Chinese and foreign teaching in one, it will be found that the new addition made to his powers as a healer will be by no means small. From the near he will be able to reach the distant. The world will be the better for it. Men will live longer and the advantage gained will be in truth incalculable. Such is the view of foreign medicine held by Viceroy Li at the present time. He thinks he finds the western doctrine of the nerves in the old medical treatises of his country. Statements on anatomy made by modern Europeans he fancies agree with the Han commentator Chêng's views in his notes to the *Chow-li*. As to the description of the system of blood-vessels connected with the heart and liver and other parts, it may be viewed as an addition of positive utility to the native description of the same. The theory is as beautiful as it is new and it takes the learner into fields of knowledge which the Emperors Shun and Yü never traversed in the days of yore. He notices that Buddhism and Taoism have both had influence on Chinese medicine, and there can be no question that alchemy has had full liberty in developing it. As to Indian influence, the anatomical statue in copper five feet high brought many centuries ago from Nepaul, and marked for teaching anatomy, is an indisputable witness, for it is kept at the hall of the Imperial Board of Physicians.

THE CHINESE *QUEUE.*

A BUDDHIST work of twelve hundred years ago by a Chinese author says that in Djambudwipa, that is in Asia, the clothing of the inhabitants varies to a large extent, and the custom of shaving off the hair and beard exists in some regions, while elsewhere hair is worn divided into two pendent *queues.* There are also countries where all the hair is shaved off except that at the crown, which is tied into one *queue.* This author also mentions that some nations pluck out the hair entirely, while others cut it short. Some people, he says, let the hair flow loose down on the shoulders while others prefer to plait it. In some instances the front hair is plaited and the back hair left loose. A thousand years passed away and the Tartar custom, which this author described as an outlandish novelty, became the custom of all China. The crown was left but all the rest of the hair was shaven. This became the national custom at the Manchu conquest about A.D. 1644. It did not become the rule in China to shave off the hair all round the crown from any religious motive but simply by military compulsion. You have to obey orders, said the conquerors, sword in hand. If you refuse to shave according to the Tartar custom you must die, for refusal will constitute you a rebel. So the change was made from the north-east province as the conquest proceeded, till the whole nation had their heads shaved except the crown. The Mongols when they conquered China did not act in this way. in the 13th century, but allowed the Chinese to dress their hair with a comb in the national way, while they themselves wore a central *queue* and shaved round the crown, like the Manchus of to-day.

If it be asked why did the Tartars shave, the reply will probably be correct that the custom began in religion and was continued for cleanliness, for fashion's sake and for the comfort of the skin. That religion was the originating cause is likely, because in India with the spread of Buddhism the shaving of the entire head became very common. This was in pursuance of a vow to forsake the world. The monastic vow of the Buddhists requires abandonment of worldly enjoyments, and luxuries. To drink wine and eat flesh are both forbidden. People prided themselves on their hair and therefore that must go also. The monk and nun must truly forsake the world. The entire loss of the hair is requisite for every one who gives himself in cordial devotion to Buddha, the law, and the priesthood. In the case of every Buddhist the shaving of the entire head is the fruit of a religious vow, professedly made with the most serious and desired act of will to forsake the world. It is only dispensed with when he takes a greater vow, that of the long-haired ascetic. Buddhism opens the way to a succession of stages in the religious life, and he who wears his hair unshorn has reached a higher grade than the shaven crowd of monks who chant their prayers together in praise of Buddha in the sacred hall of their temple. Such a man lives alone and gives himself to high meditation. His wearing his hair unshorn is a sign that he is too absorbed in thought to attend to the adornment of the body. This and other customs of the Buddhists have, it may be said, been silent witnesses to the rest of the Chinese of the importance of the Buddhist spiritual teaching. The complete shaving of head and beard of the common Buddhist, and unshaven hair of the hermits who are bound by the higher vows, have been symbols from which Buddhism desired that all neophytes should learn the importance of the spiritual and the eternal, and the inferiority of the material and the evanescent.

But the tonsure did not begin with the Buddhists. It began in south-western Asia, that wonderful centre of the world's great movements of thought, or in Egypt, early distinguished for its civilisation. The Egyptian priests were completely shorn and from them the habit of shaving off hair and beard extended to the laity. Only the women always wore their own hair, and they

were not shaved even in mourning or after death. Shaving was universal among the men, but the hair and beard were allowed to grow in times of mourning. They wore wigs instead of their natural hair, and they had a wig for the chin which could be put on and taken off at pleasure like the wig they wore on the head. Shaving began with religion and ended with its being adopted as necessary to cleanliness and civilisation. The ancient Greeks visited Egypt and adopted Egyptian customs and we see the result in the way in which they treated the hair. They combined the religious idea with that of civilisation and cleanliness, and they added, as they would be likely to do, the notion that part of the hair should be retained for ornamental purposes. Each young man of respectable parentage when he became sixteen or seventeen cut off his hair as an offering to the gods. The commonness of this custom in ancient Greece and Rome is certain evidence that a religious motive influenced the ordinary population in removing the natural hair by cutting or shaving. They carried away the hair to dedicate it to some river god or to the temple of some divinity locally worshipped. At Rome the Vestal Virgins cut their hair short on taking their vows. At the present time in the Papal Church nuns do so too on taking the veil. Our own cutting of the hair originated with that of the Greeks and Romans, that is to say it began in certain religious considerations and then passed under certain civilising and artistic conditions. The religious significance is lost entirely now. It would naturally be the Greeks who would first study into what graceful forms the human hair may be dressed, and we can judge of their success by the sculptured heads of gods and goddesses in the museums and sculpture galleries of Europe. The hair has a conventional form in the case of every god and goddess. Hercules is distinguished by short curling locks thickly growing over every part of the head and beard.

The Greeks saw a peculiar suitability in this sort of hair for a demigod with strength of muscle in the arms and vigour of expression in the face. Jupiter is very different. He had the lion's hair and majestic attitude and expression. Neptune's locks hung dripping down perpendicularly, on each side of his face. Each goddess had a *coiffure* of her own and the sculptor always conformed his work to the conventional shaping which the characteristics of the goddess required. He developed his individual genius always within the conventional lines.

In Far Asia there has not been much development æsthetically in the same way. But as to the satisfaction felt by the immense Chinese race in losing this natural ornament by the shaving process three times a month or oftener, there seems little doubt. They do not show a desire to return to their ancient fashion. In British and Dutch colonies and all foreign countries the Chinese still shave as a rule, nor do they desire a change. Yet Doolittle tells us that at Foochow at the time of the Manchu conquest, small presents were given to Chinese who shaved. The system of pecuniary rewards was adopted to aid in the carrying out of the law. Many were most unwilling to adopt the Manchu fashion. At last the new law prevailed, and the whole population in that city fell in with the new arrangement. Only the Taoist priests and the women are now allowed to wear their hair in the old fashion.

TARTARS AS SOVEREIGNS.

THE Emperor of China is a Tartar and speaks his native language and Chinese. The King of Corea and the Emperor of Japan are really of Tartar descent, as is shown by the languages of those countries. The Shah of Persia is a Tartar by descent and so was the Great Mogul whom England dispossessed of his throne in Delhi. Proceeding farther west, the sovereign of the Turkish empire and the Khedive of Egypt are of Tartar descent

and speak a Tartar tongue. The number of Tartar sovereigns does not cease till we arrive at Morocco on the shores of the Atlantic. All through these countries not only are the sovereigns Tartar, but a large proportion of the civil service and the holders of government posts, the judges and the magistrates, are also of Tartar descent, and each of such Tartar governors, pashas, premiers, or magistrates impresses his personal characteristics on the administration during his tenure of office in the sphere he occupies as the case may be. The Daimios of old Japan are the remaining representatives of an effete feudalism and they correspond to Mongol and Turkish chiefs of clans in Tartary. Now if we were to sum up the intellectual and civilised force of all the Tartar sovereigns over the immense extent of country that has been just indicated with that of all chiefs of tribes and all magistrates high and low, with those belonging to the civil and military services of the countries embraced in this enumeration, we should have a measure of the influence now being exerted on the civilised world by the Tartar mind. That mind was trained and developed in the steppes of Russia and Siberia and on the plains of Tartary, on the shores of the Oxus and Jaxartes near the Caspian Sea, or upon the banks of the Obi and Jenissei flowing into the Polar Ocean. The ancestors of the many Tartar reigning families of to-day used to tend their cattle and sheep in the grassy glades of the Altai mountains or on the boundless green plains north of China's Great Wall or in the fertile valleys which lead from the great central plateau eastward to the coast of the Pacific Ocean or on the shores of the Blue Sea in Tibet.

Intellectually the Tartar races have not been creative. Their literature has had no signal development, their historians have limited their scope, their poets have been chiefly alliterative, like those of Mongolia, or simply lyrical like those of Japan. The Tartars in China have undoubted capacity and intellectual respectability, suiting them for taking part in the administration and giving important aid to the ruling family in guiding the vessel of the state. The same thing is noticeable in Japan. The competency of the native statesmen in that country is beyond question. The prudence they have shown when there was any crisis has been conspicuous. Their friendliness in negotiation with foreign States has accorded with the best teachings of modern political wisdom. Their encouragement of native and foreign trade, their introduction of railways and their adoption of other foreign improvements are proof of real enlightenment. So also their avoidance of a struggle with Christianity and their uniformly declining to defend one religion at the expense of another remind us of the emperor Akbar's liberality of disposition in governing India. But neither Turks, Japanese, Mongols nor Manchus have been creative in literature and where they have made progress they have derived inspiration from foreign sources. What Chinese training has done for Japanese authorship, Persian and Arab training has done for Turkish and Mongolian authorship. Neither the Buddhist classics nor the Koran have so elevated the Tartar races as to lead to the growth among them of a vigorous native literature. The Mongols are fond of Buddhist stories, and the Turks of Arabian stories. They delight to while away the hours of the long evenings with the recital of religious romances. But they are not creatively great and do not covet a thorough training of the mental faculties.

The question why the Tartar races should have been, as proved by history, able to control men and to make conquests in a way extraordinarily successful is to be answered by giving attention to their mode of life. They live in the saddle, they are accustomed to swift locomotion. They are all divided into tribes and the tribesmen are accustomed to obey the chief's orders. The chiefs easily learn the art of command

because they frequently see before them squadrons of cavalry arranged in troops and companies under their own control. They are accustomed from their youth to direct the evolutions of cavalry, and when they fight they expect to conquer by irresistible movements of armed horsemen. Agriculturists and foot-soldiers are for want of training unable to cope with them, and are easily thrown into disorder. It is the nomad life and the habit of watching and controlling equestrian movements on a plain which may be supposed to have imparted to the Tartars the power to conquer bodies of foot-soldiers in battle. Such a gift is partly hereditary and partly acquired. The extraordinary activity of the Khirgiz when engaged in breaking in wild horses is well known. They are completely successful in a very short time in taming the wildest animals. The exercise of this wonderful faculty which they possess is described in a very interesting way in the Rev. J. G. Wood's "Dominion of Man over Animals." It is clear from the facts collected by Russian observers that the Khirgiz horse-tamer has his eyesight and muscular power improved by heredity as well as by acquired dexterity. All this additional energy which the Tartar gains by the tribal descent and the teaching he derives from the environment of his daily life was utilised by Turkish and Mongol conquerors who overwhelmed so many empires from the time of Gengis Khan onwards to the establishment of the Mongol empire in India.

We know what the Tartars have been in ancient and modern times by Chinese and European history and by th narratives of travellers. They have conquered nations more civilised than themselves in many successive instances. The Huns won Hungary A.D. 311, two centuries after that rich country had been in part settled by Roman colonies under the Emperor Trajan. Hordes of Tartars conquered North China at the end of the fourth century and retained it for 200 years. In the thirteenth century the Mongols conquered Persia and they were preceded and followed by Turkish dynasties. There has never been a purely native Persian dynasty since. The Turks afterwards conquered India, Syria, the Greek Empire and all North Africa. The long period during which they have reigned over these countries shows that they have very considerable governing ability or they would have been early displaced by other races. The Turks have improved their mental energy by inter-marriages with superior races. In this way they have appropriated the intellectual power of Europeans. It is also the habit of Tartar monarchs to select the ablest of their many sons to receive the sovereignty in succession on the death of the parent. The father's will determines who shall be heir, and it is not necessarily the eldest who ascends the vacant throne. This mode of controlling the succession secures more capable monarchs. The modern spirit is now producing a liberality unknown in the past in the institutions of Japan. It is the first instance of parliamentary institutions having been adopted by a people of Tartar race. They have never before in any country had any but a despotic monarchy.

LOCAL DISTURBANCES.

THE Kolao Hui will never emerge into any great importance because its antecedents are not encouraging. In the year 1875, says a memorial of the Viceroy Shên Pao-chêng, there was an edict directed expressly against this secret society. This was in consequence of a memorial by Li Han-chang, the present Viceroy of Canton, who had drawn the Emperor's attention to the operations of the society. The Emperor said there was no need of special rules on the subject. The governors and viceroys only required to order the local magistrates to employ either their thief-catchers or the military in apprehending offenders. It was decided at that time that it would not be advisable to punish every member of the society with death.

This would be to occasion too much bloodshed. Only the chief offenders should be proceeded against, while their followers should be scattered and separated. At the same time every care must be used to sift the charges brought against the incriminated. Great pains must be taken not to allow chief offenders to escape or punishment to fall upon the wrong persons. It was felt at that time that if this society were let alone for fear of trouble the small cockatrice might become a terrible serpent. This seems to have been realised during the present year. Along with the Kolao Hui at the time was mentioned the Anching Tao, an Anhui society, which also gave much anxiety to the authorities during several centuries and again at the beginning of the present reign and may still do so. The course to be followed was, it was then decided, the same with both. The existing machinery of the law was to be used, and no other introduced. Shên, the Viceroy of those days, agreed in opinion with Tsêng Kuo-fan, his predecessor, that the secret society men must in each case be proceeded against as ordinary criminals of the rebel or robber class.

Here we may notice that both these eminent Viceroys were agreed in thinking that the Kolao Hui people must be prosecuted without favour and by the ordinary legal methods. They had no special prestige or privilege, and there is no thought of their being secretly seconded by officials high in office, all of whom know the existence of this edict. This seems to shut out any prospect of wide support to these secret societies in influential quarters at the present time. If offenders of secret societies are not vigorously prosecuted, it is not because sympathy is felt for their aims and plans by officials, but for other reasons. Among these other reasons in the case of city magistrates comes in the consideration of expense attendant on any sort of interference in local disturbances great or small. The city magistrates of China have thief-catchers at their disposal, but usually these men are not in receipt of regular pay. If there is a robbery or disturbance the magistrate sends them to make search and must supply money for their temporary support, and so with local spies who may have special information on the whereabouts of robbers. They must be paid for their knowledge and guidance. When the local disturbance is of a larger kind and beyond the power of the magistrate's thief-catchers to manage, soldiers must be asked for. The soldiers have to be paid for their assistance whether they belong to the class of regulars or are trained braves. It is therefore an inducement to the magistrate to do without soldiers if he can, and as long as he can, because the necessary outlay is larger for the help of soldiers than for that of local thief-catchers. When the local trouble yields to inquiry and the disturbers are discovered, it is quite possible that the Viceroy or the Governor may by law order the accused to be sent to his tribunal, and the expense of sending them falls on the magistrate, if the accused changes his confession into a plea of not guilty. To be a magistrate near the provincial capital is much desired by the qualified candidates. A case of robbery may occur, for instance in the province of Kiangsu, at some city north of the Yangtze. This involves much extra expense and responsibility to the magistrate, and such a post is very unpopular among the candidates. In such a position the temptation is strong not to mention the robbery in reports to superiors and in certain cases to release the perpetrators. "This is the only thing I could do," says the magistrate, or "it was only kind to let the poor men go after the fright they had undergone, and heaven will reward me for it." Another thing the Viceroy mentions is that magistrates are changed too often. It may not be after five days, as used to happen, it is said, in the Sung dynasty, but a change may be made very frequently. Magistrates hold a post too often for a year and then go. The Viceroy says this is very unwise.

Good men should be chosen and they should hold the post for three years. This would be better for the *morale* of the service, and the people would respect the magistrates more. They would then be more able to search to the bottom of the troubles caused by the secret societies and the root of the Kolao Hui might not hold its place with such tenacity. If the place where the robbery has occurred is at a distance from the *yamén* of the Viceroy or Governor, these high authorities should be empowered to order the conveyance of criminals to the cities where the prefects and superintendents reside. Let them judge the case and if necessary pass a sentence of decapitation. Viceroy Shên would simplify the legal process by deciding it in this way. He was an able and very polite man, and it appears from what he then said in memorialising the throne, that he would urge increased care in selecting city magistrates, and when a good man is found give him his post for three years successively. He would also allow increased power to Prefects and Taotais, so that cases of criminals convicted of robbery (and these include all riots as the Chinese law shows) should be decided summarily by them to save delay and expense. He does not see in the Kolao Hui any more patriotism than in any other secret society, but merely a disturbing force which has to be put down by law. Unfortunately he does not take note of the evil resulting from the want of a paid constabulary force attached to every *yamén*. He does not remark on the impossibility of expecting prompt interference with disorder when it cannot be done except with the help of voluntary police, whose energy is made conditional on the amount of temporary rewards given to them or promised. These voluntary thief-catchers are successful often, as the name implies, in catching thieves, but with robberies on a large scale they are unable to cope. They are good as detectives but cannot suppress a riot. This, however, is from want of drill and the power to act in concert and with presence of mind. If China should ever adopt the idea of a paid constabulary, a large number of these irregular detectives would probably join such a force, allured by the prospect of monthly pay, and their efficiency would be greatly improved by drill and regular habits, if they could in any way be freed from opium smoking. It would be an immense advantage to the country if the police force could be so strengthened as to check the great tendency to live by plunder existing in many provinces. It would then be possible to ameliorate the criminal law. Executions would be less common and life regarded as more secred. With a drilled constabulary and a civilised system of jail confinement, the Viceroys would not be asking for power to decapitate being granted to Prefects and Taotais. They could ask only for extension of the system of a drilled constabulary, for the protection of each neighbourhood from all forms of piracy and robbery, to be maintained by local rates. There is nothing impracticable in an improvement of this nature.

www.ingramcontent.com/pod-product-compliance
Lightning Source LLC
Chambersburg PA
CBHW022035080426
42733CB00007B/835